DISCOVERING YOUR IDENTITY
IN CHRIST

CHARLES
STANLEY

THOMAS NELSON PUBLISHERS
Nashville

Copyright © 1999 by Charles Stanley

All rights reserved. Written permission must be secured from the publisher to use or reproduce any part of this book, except for brief quotations in critical reviews or articles.

Published in Nashville, Tennessee, by Thomas Nelson, Inc.

Scripture quotations are from THE NEW KING JAMES VERSION. Copyright © 1979, 1980, 1982, Thomas Nelson, Inc., Publishers.

ISBN 0-7852-7288-7

Printed in the United States of America
04 05 06 07   05 04 03 02 01 00

CONTENTS

Introduction: You Are a Saint!   v
1. A Fresh Look at Your Identity As a Believer   1
2. In Christ   10
3. Chosen by God   21
4. Beloved Child   31
5. Redeemed   40
6. Heir   55
7. Enlightened Saint   66
8. Member of the Body   79
9. Holy Vessel for Ministry   91
10. God's Masterpiece   101
    Conclusion: Believe for God's Best   109

YOU ARE A SAINT!

How do you see yourself?

Do you regard yourself as a saint today?

Each of us acts on the basis of how we *see* ourselves. Our opinion of self directs and focuses our behavior every hour of every day. If we have a faulty self-image—which is having any self-image other than what God says about us—we behave in a way that is contrary to God's highest purposes and plan for our lives.

Not only is having a correct self-image important to the way we make personal choices, deal with crises and problems, and approach various tasks and challenges in life, but a correct self-image impacts the way we deal with other people.

Jesus taught that we are to love our neighbors *as we love ourselves.* In other words, we are to love, appreciate, regard, value, and treat others in the same way that we love, appreciate, regard, value, and treat ourselves. If we do *not* love ourselves in an appropriate way, we cannot love others as God desires for us to love them. A healthy, God-based self-image is vital if we are going to relate to others in a truly Christlike way.

The Basis for Your Sainthood

The Bible says that those who believe in Christ Jesus and who have accepted Him as their Savior and are seeking to follow Him as their Lord are *saints.* Each of us must choose to believe what the Bible says. Do you *believe* today that you are a saint?

Being a saint is not based upon how you *feel*. Most of us do not feel like saints at any given hour on any given day. Feelings come and go. Emotions rise and fall. What we feel is often highly unpredictable, and emotions are certainly not a basis for making decisions about one's identity. For some people, an unruly hairdo or a spilled cup of coffee can ruin a day emotionally. No—emotions are not the basis on which we conclude that we are saints.

Being a saint is not based upon how much we *understand* about sainthood. Few people can truly say that they understand fully what it means to be a follower of Christ. None of us can fully explain the mystery of why God would choose to love us, forgive us, extend mercy and grace to us, or send His Son to die for us on the cross. A finite mind can never understand the infinite wisdom and power of almighty God. No—understanding is not the basis on which we conclude we are saints.

Being a saint is also not based upon what others say about us. You may have had people say to you, "Oh, you are a real saint!" when what they really mean is, "You are truly a kind person, a noble person, a generous person, or a helpful person." From the biblical point of view, sainthood has nothing to do with what a person *does* in the form of good works or kind gestures. Sainthood is bestowed upon those who believe in Christ on the basis of *what Jesus Christ has done.* The opinions of others are irrelevant and of no consequence.

So what qualifies a person to be a saint? Only one thing is required: that a person accept—receive, believe, and personally embrace—the sacrificial, atoning death of Jesus Christ on the cross. Our relationship with Jesus Christ is what qualifies us to be saints. Nothing else is required.

Within the concept of sainthood, however, we find a number of other truths. What does it truly *mean* to be a saint? How do saints live out their lives? What do saints do? These are the questions that are at the heart of this Bible study. When you acknowledge that you are a saint—a believer in Jesus Christ— you are only at the starting point for discovering *who you are in Christ.*

A "Right" Self-Esteem

We hear a great deal about self-esteem today. Countless books have been written on the subject and nearly all of them are aimed at helping a person *raise* low self-esteem to achieve a *good* self-esteem.

Too High. People tend to fall into two broad categories. First, there are some who have self-esteem that is too high. This is a relatively small percentage of people, in my opinion, especially since many of those who *act* as if they think too highly of themselves are actually masking a low self-image. The person with too-high self-esteem is a person who is proud, arrogant, has no regard for others, and who is totally self-centered. Such a person believes that the entire universe revolves around himself or herself. He or she has very little, if any, use for God. Too-high self-esteem leads a person to conclude, "I can make it on my own if everybody else will just get out of my way." The "Big I" operates in full force.

Too Low. Second, there are those who have self-esteem that is too low, which seems to include a large percentage of people, in my opinion. Most people look around and conclude, "I'm not good enough; I'm not capable enough; I'm not valuable; I'm worthless." They see themselves as without purpose or desirability. They cannot comprehend that another person might love them or count them as valuable, much less that God can love them.

In many cases, those with too-low self-esteem adopt a false humility—false in that their humility is not before God but, rather, before others. They say, "I can't do what you can do; I can't succeed as much as that person can succeed; I couldn't possibly be as effective as another person in this role or in doing that job or ministry." In their low self-esteem they become doormats for others to walk upon, and in the end, they often are frustrated, discouraged, depressed, and without hope for their futures.

What we don't often realize about people with too-low self-esteem is that they also see the world through the filter of their own self and their own lack of ability. They are just as guilty of the "Big I" syndrome as those with too-high self-esteem.

The Error of Comparison

There is one great error that people with both too-low and too-high self-esteem make. They are *comparing themselves to others*. God never calls us to compare ourselves with anyone! We each have been given a unique, one-of-a kind, irreplaceable purpose in God's plan. We have been created *as we are* by a loving God who desires for us to fulfill the purpose that *He* has for our lives. It is when we compare ourselves to others that we say, "I'm not like that person" and then conclude, "I'm not as good" or in some cases, "I'm so much better."

Comparison separates and divides us from one another, but of even greater consequence is the fact that comparison leads us to false conclusions about ourselves and, therefore, faulty behavior.

When we think we are better than others, we treat them as inferior, unworthy, or as failures. When we think we are not as good or valuable as others, we treat them with undue deference, resentment, frustration, and envy. Both sets of behavior keep us from loving others fully or appreciating the fullness of *who* God made them to be.

"Right" Self-Esteem

What God calls us to is neither a too-high or too-low self-esteem. He does not deal in terms of high self-esteem being "good" self-esteem. God wants us to have a *right* self-esteem. A correct self-image can never be rooted in comparison with others. It can never be concluded on the basis of what others think about us, say to us, or even the way we feel about ourselves. A correct self-image is based upon what *God* says about us in His Word.

Correct self-esteem is totally opposite to the "Big I" syndrome. Correct self-esteem says that I do not know myself fully . . . but God does. Correct self-esteem says that I cannot determine my own goodness or achieve my own forgiveness and righteousness . . . but I can accept what Jesus Christ has done on my behalf, and, therefore, become who God enables me to be by the power of the Holy Spirit dwelling in me. Correct self-esteem concludes that I do not have the ability to love others unconditionally in my own strength . . . but that I can love others as God helps me to love them.

What *God* says about our identity is generally totally opposite to what the world says. The world says, "You have to make your own success." God says, "Have a relationship with Me, trust Me, and I will give you total fulfillment and satisfaction." The world says, "If you don't make your own way and proclaim your own greatness, you'll be run over or disregarded by others." God says, "The greatest among you will become the servant of all, and in that, I will be well pleased with you." The world says, "Get all you can so you can become all you are." God says, "Give away all that you can so that you can gain your own soul."

God's desire for us is that we look to *Him* for our self-definition and for our identity.

Perhaps the most important question we each can ask ourselves at the outset of this study is this: *To whom am I looking for my self-identity, my self-image, my self-worth, my self-definition?*

Are you relying on your parents? Many people are still listening to "old tapes" of what their parents said to them when they were children. Some of those tapes are faulty!

Are you relying on a spouse, other family members, or friends to define you? If so, you need to recognize that their understanding of you is limited—and in some cases, they really don't know the real you at all! Their motives in defining you may not always be pure; their love may not always be unconditional.

Are you relying on a boss, a teacher, or another person in a position of authority to define you? If so, that person neither knows you fully nor has the ability to see into either your past or your future clearly and with absolute wisdom.

The only reliable source of accurate, wise, eternal information about you is God. He alone loves you unconditionally, understands you fully, and knows the fullness of purpose that He has built into your life and that He will help bring to pass as you trust Him.

If you are ever going to discover your *true* identity in Christ Jesus—if you are going to discover fully what it means to be a *saint*—you must turn to God and to God's Word.

I encourage you to reflect on these questions as you prepare for this study:

- *In what ways have you been relying upon others to give you a sense of self-worth or to define your identity?*

  _____

  _____

- *What is it that you believe God desires for you to understand about your identity as a believer?*

  _____

  _____

- *Are you living today in the fullness of the identity of a "saint"? What is holding you back?*

  _____

  _____

ONE

A FRESH LOOK AT YOUR IDENTITY AS A BELIEVER

Every person has an outlook on the world and on life—a way of looking at things, valuing things, judging things. We need to recognize that our perspective is something we have learned. Many of us may have adopted a wrong understanding about certain things, including the identity we have as believers in Christ Jesus.

I have found in my years of ministry that many Christians don't truly know who they are in Christ. They have misconceptions about why God forgives, what salvation means to our life on this earth, and about who God has called them to be.

In order to gain the right perspective on our identity as believers—indeed, on our full identity as human beings—we need to go to the Word of God and stay there. Various books on self-esteem and self-worth may be helpful to some, but only if the foundation of self-identity is firmly established on what the Word of God says. The Bible is God's foremost communication on the subject of self-esteem and self-identity. It is the reference to which we must return continually to discover who we are, and, on the basis of who we are, how we are to respond to life's situations and to other people. Our perspective is wrong any time it doesn't match up with God's eternal truth.

As you work your way through this study guide, I encourage you to look up the references that are cited and to make notes about them in the margins of your Bible. It is far more important that you write God's insights in your Bible, which you read regularly, than to write in this book, although places are provided for you to make notes.

Keys to This Study

You will be asked at various points to respond to the material presented by answering one or more of these questions:

1. What new insights have you gained?
2. Have you ever had a similar experience?
3. How do you feel about this?
4. In what way are you feeling challenged to act?

Insights

A spiritual insight occurs when you read a passage of Scripture and the meaning of that passage suddenly becomes crystal clear to you, or you have new understanding about the passage and how it applies to your life. You may have studied, read, or meditated on that particular passage many times. But then, God reveals a new level of meaning to you. That's a spiritual insight.

Ask God to give you insights. I believe He will answer that prayer and give you insights every time you read His Word.

Insights are usually personal, and they often relate to a particular experience you have had in the past or that you are currently going through. In this way, God's Word is always timely, even as it is eternal.

I encourage you to make notes about your insights. You'll be able to review your insights later in the light of still other Scriptures that you read or that the Lord brings to your mind. You'll also have your insights more readily available for sharing with others as opportunities arise. Most people discover that they experience more insights if they are looking and listening for them in an intentional, focused way.

From time to time, you will be asked in this study guide to note what specific passages of the Bible say to you. That will be your opportunity to record your insights.

Experiences

We each come to God's Word from a unique background. What you read is filtered to a degree by your past experiences—the same thing is true for every person in your study group. Every person seems to have times when he says, "I know that particular truth in the Bible is real because of what happened to me."

To a degree, we each *are* what we have experienced—we are the product of our past environments, relationships, situations, and events. For many people, self-esteem and self-identity are directly related to specific events and experiences in the past.

What we are challenged to do as believers is to see God's hand at work in all things. Romans 8:28 tells us, "We know that all things work together for good to those who love God, to those who are the called according to His purpose." It is as we begin to believe that God can use *any* experience for our ultimate and eternal good, that even the worst experiences in our past take on new meaning.

The more we see the Bible as relating to our personal experiences, the more the Bible confirms, encourages, challenges, and convicts us as to who we are and how, therefore, we are to live our lives in the future. Just as our past experiences determine to a degree what we think about ourselves, so what we believe about ourselves determines to a degree our future experiences. It is as we come to see the Bible directly impacting and relating to our personal lives, and as we begin to make choices to conform our lives to what the Bible says, that we experience the renewal of our minds and grow in our ability to reflect Christ to the world.

God's Word is universal, as well as individual and personal, and there isn't anything we experience as human beings that isn't addressed by the Bible in one or more ways. The Bible is about people and about God's relationship to people—set in the context of time and experiences. The Bible tells us how God works in and through situations to speak to people and to build a relationship with them. It is the richest resource possible for discovering meaning in all of life's many events and situations.

As you share your experiences in your journey of faith, you will grow spiritually. Even if you are doing this study on your own, I encourage you to talk to others about your faith experiences. Most people discover that as they share faith experiences they grow in their understanding of how God is working in their lives and how He uses experiences to mold us into the image of Christ Jesus.

Emotional Responses

Just as we have unique sets of experiences, we also have our own emotional responses to God's Word. No one emotional response is right or more valid than another. One person may be frightened or puzzled by what he reads, another may feel relief or joy.

The fact is, the Bible has an emotional impact on us. What we read in the Bible sometimes moves us to tears. At other times we may feel great elation, sorrow, hope, longing, love, surprise, or conviction. God made us as human beings to have emotions, and He expects us to have an emotional response to His Word, just as we have an emotional response to Him and to other people, books, movies, plays, and situations.

Face your emotional responses to the Bible honestly. Learn to share your emotions with others.

As you share life experiences and your emotions related to God's Word, keep in mind that neither our experiences nor our emotions make the Bible true. The Bible is truth, period. The reason we look at our experiences and identify our feelings is so that we might face our lives honestly in the light of God's truth. It is as we take a look at our feelings that we often see how the Lord is working in us and how He may desire for us to pursue additional avenues of study. For example, if you are puzzled by what you read, and if you recognize that you are perplexed, you will likely want to know why you feel that way. Your emotional response can lead you to find answers that you might not originally have intended to seek out. Or, if you feel fear or sorrow at what you read, and if you are honest about those emotions, you are more likely to search out the reasons for your fear or sorrow. You may uncover areas in your own past, or misteachings you have had about God's Word, that have impacted your self-identity and self-worth.

Allow the Scriptures to touch you emotionally. See your emotions as a springboard for moving into a deeper relationship with the Lord.

Do not, however, allow feelings expressed in a group study to sidetrack you from your purpose, which is a study of God's Word. Do not become so introspective about feelings that you allow feelings to become the focus of your conversation. Always bring feelings back into line with what the Bible says. Do not allow your group study to become a group-therapy type of session. Stay in the Word.

Challenges

God intends for us to be challenged by His Word each and every day of our lives. He has a purpose in communicating with us. He wants us always to be growing more and more like His Son, Jesus Christ. Real growth comes not in merely understanding God's Word, but in applying it. As James wrote, "Be doers of the word, and not hearers only" (James 1:22).

Perhaps more so in a study of self-identity than in any other study, you are going to be confronted repeatedly with an opportunity to readjust the way you think about yourself. You may find yourself saying often, "I know that's what God's Word says, but that isn't how I have thought about myself" or, "I now know what God says about me—how can I change the way I think about myself?" Statements such as those lie at the starting point of *change* and *growth*. Don't back away from the challenge!

As you read and study God's Word, pinpoint and define, as best you can, specific areas in which you believe God is challenging you to change the perspective you have about yourself. Ask yourself often, "What is the next step God has for me to take? How can I begin to walk in and to manifest this change of thinking that God desires for me to have about myself?"

God desires to get you into His Word so He can get His Word into you, and in turn, so that you can share His Word with others. Many people discover in Bible study that almost immediately after they have confronted a new biblical truth, they have an opportunity to share that truth with another person in the form of loving encouragement or edification. For example, it may be a new idea to you to think of yourself as a saint. You may feel challenged at that idea and begin to ask, "How do I respond to life as a *saint*? What does God desire for me to do as a saint?" Even as you are in the process of answering those questions, don't be surprised if you have an opportunity to encourage another believer in the next few days or weeks by saying to that person, "Did you know that as a believer in Christ Jesus, *you* are a saint?" What God triggers in you is nearly always something that God also desires to trigger in other people.

As you have opportunities to discuss and share the very things you are learning in this study, be aware that God is a master of timing! Nothing is mere coincidence or happenstance with God.

Also be aware that as you experience changes in your self-identity—the definition you have of yourself and the perspective you have on life—your *behavior* is going to change, sometimes subtly and sometimes dramatically. Others are going to see these changes in you and are likely to ask you about them. Use the questions that others ask as an opportunity to be bold in sharing how the Lord is working in your life.

If you do not have somebody with whom to discuss your insights, experiences, emotions, and challenges, find somebody. Perhaps you can start a Bible study in your home. Perhaps you can talk to your pastor about organizing Bible study groups in your church. There is much to be learned on your own. There is much more to be learned as you become part of a small group that desires to grow in the Lord and to understand His Word more fully.

Keep the Bible Central

As you meet with others to study your identity in Christ, stay focused on what the Bible says. Let the Bible speak for itself. Don't get sidetracked by opinions or personal ideas. Commentaries have their place, but ultimately the Bible is a spiritual book that reflects the unfathomable riches of God's own Spirit.

Come to God's Word as if it is a banquet table from which you can eat to satisfy the full longing of your spirit for the things of God. Come expecting to have God's Word change you and cause you to develop, grow, and be equipped for the fullness of the plan and purpose God has for you. Come expecting to find your true identity in the Bible—your eternal identity, your spiritual identity.

If you are doing a personal Bible study, be diligent in keeping your focus on God's Word. Self-analysis or personal recovery is not the goal. Becoming more like Jesus Christ is the goal. All of our personal identity is ultimately related to and must be conformed to the likeness of Him. Approach your study with a genuine desire to discover yourself *in Christ*.

Prayer

I encourage you strongly to begin and end each Bible study session in prayer. Ask God to give you spiritual eyes to see what He wants you to see and spiritual ears to hear what He wants to say to you. Ask Him to bring to your mind experiences that relate to what you read, to help you clarify your feelings, and to give you new insights. Ask Him to reveal to you what He desires for you to be, say, and do.

As you end a Bible study session, ask the Lord to imprint on your heart what you have learned so you will never forget it. Ask Him to transform you into the likeness of His Son as you meditate on His Word and apply it to your daily life. Ask Him to give you courage to do what He is calling you to do. Pray for boldness to be faithful in your walk with Him and to give witness about the Lord's healing and transforming power at every opportunity presented to you.

- *What new insights about your identity as a believer in Christ Jesus are you hoping to gain from this study?*

_____

_____

- *Have you struggled in the past with issues related to your own self-identity, self-worth, or self-esteem? Have you experienced God's forgiveness in your life? Have you opened yourself up to the power of the Holy Spirit to transform you? Have you faced the fact that God's Word may present an "image" of you that you do not presently have about yourself?*

_____

_____

- *How do you feel about facing your own identity in Christ?*

_____

_____

• *Are you open to the possibility that God may desire to change some things about the way you see yourself or the perspective that you presently have on life?*

TWO

IN CHRIST

Most Christians today do not seem to know who they are. If you ask a person, "Who are you?" he or she is likely to respond with their name and then give you their place of employment or the name of a spouse or other relative as part of their identification.

One woman once said to me, "I'm Jane, wife of Tom, mother of Sally and Dennis, daughter of George and Ruth." She then went on to tell me the name of the company for which she worked. When I asked her, "But who are you as a Christian?" she stared at me blankly and finally said, "Well, I'm a member of *your church!*"

Many people give the name of a denomination or specific church for their identity as a Christian. Some believe their identity as a Christian can be summed up by saying, "I'm baptized," "I'm a regular churchgoer" or, "I've been saved for twenty-two years."

More than any other single factor, what you believe about yourself as a Christian determines your self-identity and your self-esteem. Our identity and esteem are not a matter of who we know, what kind of car we drive, where we work, which neighborhood we live in, or the friends or relatives we have. Our identity and esteem as believers are to flow from the relationship we have with God through Christ Jesus, His Only begotten Son.

It is critically important today that we know who we are in

Christ. It is only when we know *who* we are that we can properly discern

- how we are to respond—in virtually any situation.
- how we are to make decisions—in the face of virtually any problem, need, challenge, or opportunity.
- how we are to answer virtually any question posed to us.
- how we are to treat other people.
- how we are to schedule our priorities in life.
- how we are to witness about Jesus Christ.

Our identity is equally critical to the way we feel about ourselves, the hope we have for our own future, and the degree to which we believe we can or should develop our individual talents, skills, and abilities.

- *Who are you? How do you define yourself to others? In what ways do you feel challenged as you attempt to describe yourself?*

_____

_____

More than any person apart from Jesus Christ, the apostle Paul was most concerned about the true identity of the believer. And Paul's foremost statement about the believer's identity can be summed up in two words: "in Christ."

Notice the number of times Paul used this phrase, "in Christ," in the first part of his letter to the Ephesians. In fact, as you read through this passage, I invite you to circle all of the times you find the phrases "in Christ," "in Him," "in Himself," "in the Beloved" (who is Christ), and "in whom" (when it refers to Christ)!

Paul, an apostle of Jesus Christ by the will of God,
To the saints who are in Ephesus, and faithful in

Christ Jesus:

Grace to you and peace from God our Father and the Lord Jesus Christ.

Blessed be the God and Father of our Lord Jesus Christ, who has blessed us with every spiritual blessing in the heavenly places in Christ, just as He chose us in Him before the foundation of the world, that we should be holy and without blame before Him in love, having predestined us to adoption as sons by Jesus Christ to Himself, according to the good pleasure of His will, to the praise of the glory of His grace, by which He made us accepted in the Beloved.

In Him we have redemption through His blood, the forgiveness of sins, according to the riches of His grace which He made to abound toward us in all wisdom and prudence, having made known to us the mystery of His will, according to His good pleasure which He purposed in Himself, that in the dispensation of the fullness of the times He might gather together in one all things in Christ, both which are in heaven and which are on earth—in Him.

In Him also we have obtained an inheritance, being predestined according to the purpose of Him who works all things according to the counsel of His will, that we who first trusted in Christ should be to the praise of His glory.

In Him you also trusted, after you heard the word of truth, the gospel of your salvation; in whom also, having believed, you were sealed with the Holy Spirit of promise, who is the guarantee of our inheritance until the redemption of the purchased possession, to the praise of His glory. (Eph. 1:1–14)

• *What new insights do you have into this passage of Scripture?*

_____

_____

Our relationship with Christ is to be the inner motivation for our lives. It is to be our security and our confidence. So many people today are drawing their identity from the name on the label in their dress or the name stitched onto their jeans, rather than drawing their identity from where their name is written: in the Lamb's Book of Life! We are *in Christ*. If anyone asks you, "Who *are* you?" your answer should be this: "I am a believer in Christ Jesus. I am *in Christ*."

What the Word Says	**What the Word Says to Me**
Paul, called to be an apostle . . . to the church of God which is at Corinth, to those who are sanctified in Christ Jesus. (1 Cor. 1:1–2)	....
Paul and Timothy, bondservants of Jesus Christ, to all the saints in Christ Jesus who are in Philippi. (Phil. 1:1)	....
Paul, an apostle of Jesus Christ by the will of God . . . to the saints and faithful brethren in Christ who are in Colosse. (Col. 1:1–2)	....

• *How would Paul address a letter to* you *and to your study group of Christian believers today?*

_____

_____

Where Were You Before You Were in Christ?

Where were you before you were in Christ? The Bible says that you were "in Adam." You were a natural heir of Adam and Eve, the first man and woman created by God, who rebelled against God in their disobedience and who became subject to sin and spiritual death. You were born naturally with a sinful state of heart—your propensity was to sin, your desire was to sin. Nobody ever teaches a little child to steal, lie, or to covet every toy in sight. A child is born with a "me, myself, and I" complex.

Paul described this state of being "in Adam" in this way to the Ephesians:

> You He made alive, who were dead in trespasses and sins, in which you once walked according to the course of this world, according to the prince of the power of the air, the spirit who now works in the sons of disobedience, among whom also we all once conducted ourselves in the lusts of our flesh, fulfilling the desires of the flesh and of the mind, and were by nature children of wrath, just as the others. (Eph. 2:1–3)

In your sinful state, you had no way to bring about your own forgiveness or freedom from sin and guilt. No person can earn forgiveness, achieve it, accomplish it, attain it, or succeed in winning it. No person has the authority to say to himself, "You are forgiven."

A life "in Adam" is a life of darkness—blinded to the truth about God, separated from a relationship with God, and in bondage to sin's impulses—without genuine freedom to live a righteous life. It is a life headed for eternal death—the ultimate consequence of an unchanged sinful heart.

What the Word Says

"There is none righteous, no, not one;
There is none who under-stands;
There is none who seeks after God.
They have all turned aside;
They have together become unprofitable;
There is none who does good, no, not one."
"Their throat is an open tomb;
With their tongues they have practiced deceit";
"The poison of asps is under their lips";
"Whose mouth is full of curs-ing and bitterness."
"Their feet are swift to shed blood;
Destruction and misery are in their ways;
And the way of peace they have not known."
"There is no fear of God before their eyes."
(Rom. 3:10–18, quoting from Pss. 14:1–3; 53:1–3; Eccl. 7:20; Pss. 5:9; 140:3; 10:7; 3:178; Isa. 59:7–8; and Ps. 36:1)

What the Word Says to Me

For when you were slaves of
sin . . . What fruit did you have
then in the things of which you
are now ashamed? For the end
of those things is death. (Rom.
6:20–21)

At that time you were without
Christ, being aliens from the
commonwealth of Israel and
strangers from the covenants
of promise, having no hope
and without God in the world.
(Eph. 2:12)

But Now . . . In Christ!

Throughout his epistle, Paul gave a very vivid and complete description of our life "in Adam," but he never ended the story there. Paul always went on to give the hope and the great contrast of our life now as believers—a life *in Christ*. He wrote to the Ephesians, "But now in Christ Jesus you who once were far off have been brought near by the blood of Christ" (Eph. 2:13).

He also said this of the transforming mercy, love, and grace of God at work in our lives:

What the Word Says

But God, who is rich in mercy,
because of His great love with
which He loved us, even when
we were dead in trespasses,
made us alive together with
Christ (by grace you have been
saved), and raised us up

What the Word Says to Me

together, and made us sit together in the heavenly places in Christ Jesus. (Eph. 2:4–6)

But now Christ is risen from the dead, and has become the firstfruits of those who have fallen asleep. For since by man [Adam] came death, by Man [Christ Jesus] also came the resurrection of the dead. For as in Adam all die, even so in Christ all shall be made alive. (1 Cor. 15:20–22)

For the wages of sin is death, but the gift of God is eternal life in Christ Jesus our Lord. (Rom. 6:23)

The life we have in Christ was made possible at God's initiative and at Christ Jesus' death on the cross. God was motivated by love to save mankind, and He did for man what man could not do for himself—He completely and eternally bridged the gap created by man's sin so that *all* who believe in Christ Jesus might be forgiven their sins and experience eternal life. As John wrote in his Gospel:

> For God so loved the world that He gave His only begotten Son, that whoever believes in Him should not perish but have everlasting life. For God did not send His Son into the world to condemn the world, but that the world through Him might be saved. He who believes in Him is not condemned; but he who does not believe is condemned already, because he has not believed in the name of the only begotten Son of God. (John 3:16–18)

Believing and accepting the work that Jesus Christ did for us on the cross as being for our personal salvation is *all* that is required for us to exchange our old identity of being "in Adam" to our new identity of being "in Christ." It is not only *all* that is required, but it is *the* requirement. No substitution for this requirement will work—no amount of good works, no amount of self-help techniques, no amount of thinking good thoughts or striving to be a good person. Paul made it very clear: "For by grace you have been saved through faith, and that not of yourselves; it is the gift of God, not of works, lest anyone should boast" (Eph. 2:8–9).

- *What new insights do you have into your identity as a believer?*

  _____

  _____

- *How do you feel when you think back to your old life "in Adam"? How do you feel when you think about your new life "in Christ"? How do you feel about what Jesus Christ did on the cross for your sake?*

  _____

  _____

- *In what ways are you feeling challenged in your spirit?*

  _____

  _____

Our Life in Christ

Throughout the New Testament, we find a number of descriptions about what it means to be made alive "in Christ." Paul wrote this to the Corinthians:

Therefore, if anyone is in Christ, he is a new creation; old things have passed away; behold, all things have become new. Now all things are of God, who has reconciled us to Himself through Jesus Christ. (2 Cor. 5:17–18)

Once we are in Christ, no longer are we to draw from a deposit of previous good works; no longer are we to rely on our old associations and alliances; no longer are we to believe the "old lies" that have been playing in our heads since early childhood that we are worthless, unwanted, or undesirable. We are new creatures with a new life ahead—a life that is totally reconciled to God and is set on a path toward fulfillment and satisfaction in Christ Jesus.

John described our life in Christ as being that of a branch abiding in a vine. He recorded these words of Jesus:

> I am the vine, you are the branches. He who abides in Me, and I in him, bears much fruit; for without Me you can do nothing. If anyone does not abide in Me, he is cast out as a branch and is withered; and they gather them and throw them into the fire, and they are burned. If you abide in Me, and My words abide in you, you will ask what you desire, and it shall be done for you. By this My Father is glorified, that you bear much fruit; so you will be My disciples. (John 15:5–8)

- *What new insights do you have into this passage from the Gospel of John about your identity in Christ?*

The person who is in Christ is a person who will have a heart bent toward God. He will be able to receive and enjoy those things that the Lord has reserved exclusively for believers. He will be empowered to live a godly life. He will desire to seek and pursue a life that is marked by the fruit of the Holy

Spirit, who lives within the believer, and by a bold witness for Christ Jesus.

What freedom this gives us! We are not destined to receive what we deserved when we were "in Adam"—rather, we are destined to receive what God loves to give us "in Christ"! No more striving, no more climbing the ladder of acceptability, no more performing in hopes of gaining God's applause. Our new life in Christ is not based upon what we do, but on who we *are* in Christ.

- *What new insights do you have into your identity as a believer?*

  _____

  _____

- *In what ways are you feeling challenged in your spirit?*

  _____

  _____

THREE

CHOSEN BY GOD

Are you aware that as a believer in Christ Jesus, you have been chosen by God?

Chosen. What a wonderful word that is! *Chosen* is a word that automatically speaks to us of value, worthiness, love, and appreciation. To be chosen means that others *want* to be with us, *want* to know us, *want* to spend time with us. Certainly all of those things are true when it comes to God's *choosing* to be reconciled to us in Christ Jesus and choosing us as His children. In choosing us, God is saying, "I want to be in a close relationship with you; I want to spend time with you; I want to share Myself with you fully."

As a believer in Christ Jesus, not only are you a saint *in Christ,* but you have been *chosen* by God to have a very special relationship with Him.

The apostle Paul wrote to the Ephesians:

> Blessed be the God and Father of our Lord Jesus Christ, who has blessed us with every spiritual blessing in the heavenly places in Christ, just as *He chose us in Him before the foundation of the world,* that we should be holy and without blame before Him in love. (Eph. 1:3–4, emphasis mine)

- *Think back to an experience in your life when you truly felt "chosen" for something special. How did you feel? How did you respond to being "chosen"?*

_____

_____

• *How do you feel about being "chosen" by God to be a saint in Christ Jesus?*

_____

_____

God Does the Choosing

As we study what it means to be chosen by God in Christ Jesus, we must be very certain about one thing: it is God who does the choosing. Paul wrote that "He chose us in Him before the foundation of the world" (Eph. 1:4). In other words, from the very beginning of all things, God *planned* to be in relationship with you through Christ Jesus. You were always a part of God's plan and purpose, you were always chosen by God— even before you personally accepted Jesus as your Savior. You have always been a *desired* child of God.

So many children grow up being told by their parents, "We never really wanted you. You were an accident. You were a 'surprise.'" The truth from God's perspective is something entirely different: God *always* wanted you. You were part of His design and His plan from the foundation of the earth. You were intended, expected, and created by God for precisely this time and for a precise role and purpose. God didn't say when you were born, "Well, what can I do about this child?" No! God said at your birth, "This is the child I created for this specific time, place, and purpose on the earth!"

Furthermore, Paul wrote that God chose us "according to the good pleasure of His will" (Eph. 1:5). In other words, God created you because it *pleased* Him to create you.

None of us can ever fathom God's grace in choosing us. Nothing you ever did or could do put you into a position to be chosen by God. You didn't say the right things, do the right things, or become the right person. God chose you because He *wanted* to choose you and because He desired to be in relationship with you. He made a sovereign choice, totally from His own motivation of love and mercy.

"Grace" is the unmerited, undeserved favor of God at work in our lives, and we are the recipients of divine grace! Our being chosen is the act of a loving God, who willed to choose us solely because He gained pleasure in doing so.

- *In what ways are you feeling challenged about your identity in Christ?*

_____

_____

What the Word Says	What the Word Says to Me
Blessed is the nation whose God is the LORD, The people He has chosen as His own inheritance. (Ps. 33:12)	
But you are a chosen generation, a royal priesthood, a holy nation, His own special people, that you may proclaim the praises of Him who called you out of darkness into His marvelous light; who once were not a people but are now the people of God, who had not obtained mercy but now have obtained mercy. (1 Peter 2:9–10)	

Predestined to Be Adopted

In writing to the Ephesians, the apostle Paul conveyed this truth of our being "chosen" by using two very specific terms: *predestined* and *adopted*. He said about God the Father,

> He chose us in Him [Christ] before the foundation of the world . . . having *predestined* us to *adoption* as sons by Jesus Christ to Himself. (Eph. 1:4–5, emphasis mine)

Does God make choices? Yes! God *chose* Israel: "My people, My chosen. / This people I have formed for Myself; / They shall declare My praise" (Isa. 43:20–21).

God *chose* Jesus to be the Lamb slain from the foundation of the world (Rev. 13:8).

And God *chose* you to be His person on the earth today.

Many Christians seem divided on the issue of predestination. There are those who advocate "whosoever will," and they put the emphasis on man's will to choose to receive God's love and forgiveness. There are those who advocate "predestined," and they put the emphasis on God's will to choose man by pouring out His love and forgiveness as He desires. The fact is—both are correct! The invitation to receive God's forgiveness is extended to all . . . and the net result is that some are chosen.

This same Paul who spoke so clearly to the Ephesians about our being predestined had this to say about the Hebrew people, who saw themselves as the chosen people of God:

> I could wish that I myself were accursed from Christ for my brethren, my countrymen according to the flesh, who are Israelites, to whom pertain the adoption, the glory, the covenants, the giving of the law, the service of God, and the promises; of whom are the fathers and from whom, according to the flesh, Christ came, who is over all, the eternally blessed God. Amen.

But it is not that the word of God has taken no effect.

> For they are not all Israel who are of Israel, nor are they all children because they are the seed of Abraham . . . Why? Because they did not seek it by faith, but as it were, by the works of the law . . . Brethren, my heart's desire and prayer to God for Israel is that they may be saved. (Rom. 9:3–7, 32; 10:1)

Paul was the first to say that not all of Israel, the "chosen people," were predestined to salvation. He concluded, "Whoever calls on the name of the LORD shall be saved" (Rom. 10:13).

Paul invested his life in preaching the gospel to *all* with whom he had contact. As he said to the Corinthians:

> For though I am free from all men, I have made myself a servant to all, that I might win the more; and to the Jews I became as a Jew, that I might win Jews; to those who are under the law, as under the law, that I might win those who are under the law; to those who are without law, as without law (not being without law toward God, but under law toward Christ), that I might win those who are without law; to the weak I became as weak, that I might win the weak. *I have become all things to all men, that I might by all means save some. Now this I do for the gospel's sake, that I may be partaker of it with you.* (1 Cor. 9:19–23, emphasis mine)

Paul never judged any person as being unworthy of the gospel; he preached that all who heard him might accept God's forgiveness by faith and experience the fullness of God's grace in their lives.

This matter of man's free will and God's predestined choice is a matter no person can ever fully understand with the mind. It is a matter for *believing by faith*—for accepting God's Word as truth and recognizing from our present position as believers in Christ Jesus that we have been *chosen* by God to be saints in Christ.

One way of looking at this is to see that prior to our salvation and our acceptance of Christ, we each fell into the "whosoever will" category (see John 3:16). After we accept Christ, we find ourselves in the "predestined" category.

- *Can you recall experiences in which the Lord seemed to be wooing you into receiving Christ Jesus? Recall how you felt about Christ before you accepted Him as your Savior, and how you have felt since receiving God's forgiveness.*

_____

_____

What the Word Says

Peter, an apostle of Jesus Christ, to the pilgrims of the Dispersion in Pontus, Galatia, Cappadocia, Asia, and Bithynia, elect according to the foreknowledge of God the Father, in sanctification of the Spirit, for obedience and sprinkling of the blood of Jesus Christ. (1 Peter 1:1–2)

Peter said to them, "Repent, and let every one of you be baptized in the name of Jesus Christ for the remission of sins; and you shall receive the gift of the Holy Spirit. For the promise is to you and to your children, and to all who are afar off, as many as the Lord

What the Word Says to Me

....

....

....

....

....

....

....

....

....

....

....

....

....

....

....

....

....

....

our God will call." (Acts
2:38–39)

The Lord is not slack concern-
ing His promise, as some
count slackness, but is longsuffering toward us, not willing
that any should perish but that
all should come to repentance.
(2 Peter 3:9)

[Jesus said], "Many are called,
but few are chosen." (Matt.
22:14; 20:16)

Rather than focus on what might have been had you not received God's forgiveness and accepted Jesus Christ as your Savior, put your focus on *who* you are as a believer. You are a chosen saint of God, chosen from the foundation of the world.

Our Adoption

Paul further wrote that we were predestined for a very specific role: to be an adopted child of God (see Eph. 1:5).

Adoption in the time Paul was writing was a little different from what it is today. A father in Rome might disown a natural-born child, but a father could not legally disown an adopted child. Adopted children had full rights as a child to *all* that a father might leave as an inheritance and to the full use of the father's name. Adoption was highly prized in Rome because it carried with it great legal privileges and societal recognition. In a culture in which natural-born children were often overlooked, discarded, or shut out of a father's presence, adopted children were conveyed the full rights of "sonship."

Paul's goal in writing to the Ephesians was that they understand their position in Christ—God had chosen them to be *sons*. They were in a privileged position before God!

What the Word Says

When the fullness of the time had come, God sent forth His Son, born of a woman, born under the law, to redeem those who were under the law, that we might receive the adoption as sons. And because you are sons, God has sent forth the Spirit of His Son into your hearts, crying out, "Abba, Father!" Therefore you are no longer a slave but a son, and if a son, then an heir of God through Christ. (Gal. 4:4–7)

For as many as are led by the Spirit of God, these are sons of God. For you did not receive the spirit of bondage again to fear, but you received the Spirit of adoption by whom we cry out, "Abba, Father." The Spirit Himself bears witness with our spirit that we are children of God, and if children, then heirs—heirs of God and joint heirs with Christ, if indeed we suffer with Him, that we may also be glorified together. (Rom. 8:14–17)

What the Word Says to Me

....
....
....
....
....
....
....
....
....
....
....
....
....

....
....
....
....
....
....
....
....
....
....
....
....
....

• *How do you feel about being "predestined to adoption" as a child of God?*

_____

_____

• *What new insights do you have into your identity as a believer?*

_____

_____

Not a Cause for Boasting

You are a chosen saint of God, predestined from the foundation of the world as an adopted child of God. What an awesome identity you have as a believer in Christ!

But is this cause for boasting? Is this fact of our identity a reason to separate ourselves from other people or to think of ourselves more highly than those who are still "in Adam"? No!

Rather than be a cause for boasting, our identity in Christ as a chosen, adopted child should give us all the more compassion for those who are outside Christ. We should feel ourselves being even more compelled to share the gospel so that others might be among the "whosoever will" and become numbered with us who are chosen. Knowing the great privilege it is to be a chosen child of God, we should seek to bring others into fellowship with us, so that they, too, might be joint heirs with Christ of all things and the recipient of all spiritual blessings!

God hates pride wherever He finds it (see Prov. 16:18). Pride will have no place in heaven. Rather than regard our "chosen" status with pride, we are wise to come humbly before God with praise and thanksgiving at *His choosing us*, and say to Him, "Abba, Father, thank You for saving me and for choosing me to be Your child."

It is as we recognize that we are chosen that we then must choose to serve, choose to witness, and choose to praise God with every breath we take.

• *In what ways are you feeling challenged about your identity as a believer in Christ Jesus?*

_____

_____

FOUR

BELOVED CHILD

You are not only God's adopted child, but you are God's beloved child. His love for you is unconditional and unlimited!

Many people have a difficult time accepting the love of God. Others accept God's love, but place conditions on it. Why is it so important that we acknowledge and accept God's unconditional love as part of our spiritual identity? Because the degree to which we receive unconditional love is directly linked to the degree we are able to give unconditional love to others.

Do you put qualifiers on God's love?

Do you find yourself "objecting" to the fact that God loves you?

If so, you are rejecting a part of your spiritual identity as a believer—the fact that you *are* the beloved child of God.

- *How do you feel when you hear the words, "God loves you"?*

  _____

  _____

- *Have you had experiences in the past when you have felt the love of God in a significant way?*

  _____

  _____

Love Is Our Status in Christ

The apostle Paul wrote to the Ephesians that the believer is "accepted in the Beloved" (Eph. 1:6). The "Beloved," of course, is Christ Jesus. Few would argue that God the Father loved Jesus Christ, His Only begotten Son. It is inconceivable to think that a loving God would not love the Son, a member of the holy Trinity!

As believers, we are "in Christ." Our entire identity before God the Father is clothed in the righteousness and identity of Jesus Christ. We are part of the Beloved—we are loved because we are in Christ Jesus and God loves Jesus.

What the Word Says	What the Word Says to Me
When He had been baptized, Jesus came up immediately from the water; and behold, the heavens were opened to Him, and He saw the Spirit of God descending like a dove and alighting upon Him. And suddenly a voice came from heaven, saying, "This is My beloved Son, in whom I am well pleased." (Matt. 3:16–17)	....
Behold, My Servant whom I have chosen, My Beloved in whom My soul is well pleased! I will put My Spirit upon Him, And He will declare justice to the Gentiles. (Matt. 12:18, based upon Isa. 42:1)	....

In this the love of God was manifested toward us, that God has sent His only begotten Son into the world, that we might live through Him. In this is love, not that we loved God, but that He loved us and sent His Son to be the propitiation for our sins. (1 John 4:9–10)

The Characteristics of God's Love

As is the case with God's mercy, forgiveness, and grace, God's love pours from His infinite and eternal heart, at God's will. God *chooses* to love. He initiates love. He does not "react" to love; He loves *first*. As John wrote, "We love Him because He first loved us" (1 John 4:19).

Read what the apostle Paul wrote to Titus about God's love initiative:

> But when the kindness and the love of God our Savior toward man appeared, not by works of righteousness which we have done, but according to His mercy He saved us, through the washing of regeneration and renewing of the Holy Spirit, whom He poured out on us abundantly through Jesus Christ our Savior. (Titus 3:4–6)

We didn't earn the coming of Jesus Christ. We didn't "deserve" the death of God's Son on the cross. We didn't qualify ourselves to be recipients of God's kindness, love, or mercy. No! God *chose* to love us, and He continues to choose to love us.

- *Have you had an experience of loving another person unconditionally, even though that person may not have seemed "worthy" of love in the eyes of some people?*

_____

_____

God's Love Is Everlasting

The Lord spoke these words through the prophet Jeremiah:

> Yes, I have loved you with an everlasting love;
> Therefore with lovingkindness I have drawn you.
> (Jer. 31:3)

The good news about God's love is that there is nothing you can do to make God "un-love" you. So many Christians seem to think that when they sin, err, or fall short of God's plan for their lives, they disappoint God and He ceases to love them— at least temporarily. No! The fact is, there is nothing you have ever done to deserve God's love. No amount of good works, kindness, perfected personality, or charitable deeds can win God's love. God chooses to love, and the motivation rests entirely in Him. He loves because He is loving. As John wrote, "God is love" (1 John 4:8). It is God's nature to love, and His nature does not change or alter according to human behavior. Since there is nothing that you have done, or ever could do, to earn God's love, there is nothing you can ever do to stop God from loving you, not even for a moment. His love for you is _everlasting_.

- *What insights do you have into the everlasting nature of God's love for you?*

_____

_____

God Loves What God Creates

When God created you, He loved you. Stated another way, God does not create what God does not love. Everything that

God created was perceived by God to be "good"—perfect, whole, valuable, lovable. God doesn't make junk. He doesn't make messes. God creates what He considers to be worthy of His love, His tender care, and His eternal presence.

Furthermore, God does not pour out His Spirit on what God does not love. When you accepted Jesus Christ as your Savior, God immediately moved into your life by the power of the Holy Spirit and indwelled your being. God does not reside in a vessel He does not love.

Paul wrote to the Ephesians: "For by grace you have been saved through faith, and that not of yourselves; it is the gift of God, not of works, lest anyone should boast" (Eph. 2:8–9).

God is in the process of making you and fulfilling you and bringing you to the full purpose of your life. He is transforming you into the likeness of Jesus Christ. And He is doing so with tender and infinite love for you. God is fashioning you and molding you and chiseling you to be the beloved child with whom He desires to live forever.

God loves what God makes—including *you!*

What the Word Says

For God *so loved the world* that He gave His only begotten Son, that whoever believes in Him should not perish but have everlasting life. (John 3:16, emphasis mine)

Now hope does not disappoint, because the love of God has been poured out in our hearts by the Holy Spirit who was given to us. (Rom. 5:5)

What the Word Says to Me

Nothing Can Separate You from God's Love

Just as you, yourself, cannot cause God to stop loving you, so nothing else can keep God from loving you. As a believer in Christ Jesus, no outside force can cause God to stop loving you or separate you from His love. Paul was very clear in writing to the Romans:

> Who shall separate us from the love of Christ? Shall tribulation, or distress, or persecution, or famine, or nakedness, or peril, or sword? As it is written:
> "For Your sake we are killed all day long;
> We are accounted as sheep for the slaughter."
> Yet in all these things we are more than conquerors through Him *who loved us.* For I am persuaded that neither death nor life, nor angels nor principalities nor powers, nor things present nor things to come, nor height nor depth, nor any other created thing, shall be able to separate us from the love of God which is in Christ Jesus our Lord. (Rom. 8:35–39, emphasis mine)

- *What insights do you have into this passage from Romans 8?*

_____

_____

Our Response to God's Love

We are to have three responses to God's love for us.

1. Accept God's Love

First, we are to acknowledge God's love and accept it. My prayer for you is the prayer of Paul for the Thessalonians: "Now may the Lord direct your hearts into the love of God" (2 Thess. 3:5). Receive God's love. Open your heart to God as you pray, "Lord, I know You love me according to the truth of

Your Word. Help me to receive Your love fully so that I feel Your loving presence always."

2. Live in God's Love

God's love is part of God's omnipresent nature—His love is *always* flowing toward us. In the epistle of Jude we read, "Keep yourselves in the love of God, looking for the mercy of our Lord Jesus Christ unto eternal life" (Jude 21). John also wrote this: "God is love, and he who abides in love abides in God, and God in him" (1 John 4:16).

As believers in Christ Jesus, we are to nurture our understanding of God's love and seek to dwell in His love daily. Thank the Lord each morning for His love. Remind yourself often, "God loves me!"

> • *What insights do you have into how a person might "abide" in God's love daily?*

_____

_____

3. Love Others

As we fully receive and abide in God's love, we are to be vessels for God's love to be poured out to others. Loving others is not just a nice idea. It is a commandment of God. Jesus said,

> This is My commandment, that you love one another as I have loved you. Greater love has no one than this, than to lay down one's life for his friends. (John 15:12–13)

What the Word Says	What the Word Says to Me
And now I plead with you, lady, not as though I wrote a new commandment to you, but that which we have had	

from the beginning: that we
love one another. (2 John 5)

If someone says, "I love God,"
and hates his brother, he is a
liar; for he who does not love
his brother whom he has seen,
how can he love God whom he
has not seen? And this commandment we have from Him:
that he who loves God must
love his brother also. (1 John
4:20–21)

If we love one another, God
abides in us, and His love has
been perfected in us. (1 John
4:12)

Since you have purified your
souls in obeying the truth
through the Spirit in sincere
love of the brethren, love one
another fervently with a pure
heart. (1 Peter 1:22)

Finally, all of you be of one
mind, having compassion for
one another; love as brothers,
be tenderhearted, be courte-
ous; not returning evil for evil
or reviling for reviling, but on
the contrary blessing, knowing
that you were called to this,
that you may inherit a blessing.
(1 Peter 3:8–9)

Experiencing More of God's Love

Those who abide in God's love and are always seeking to express God's love to others are those who, in turn, will experience even *more* of God's love in their lives. This does not mean that God loves them more; God's love is infinite and eternal at all times. Rather, it means that those who seek to abide in love and who are expressing love *experience* God's love in their own lives in increasingly profound, meaningful, and joyful ways. Paul wrote about this to the Ephesians:

> I bow my knees to the Father of our Lord Jesus Christ . . . that Christ may dwell in your hearts through faith; that you, being rooted and grounded in love, may be able to comprehend with all the saints what is the width and length and depth and height—to know the love of Christ which passes knowledge; that you may be filled with all the fullness of God. (Eph. 3:14, 17–19)

If you truly desire to *feel* more of God's love and to grow in your love relationship with God, receive God's love by faith, choose to abide in God's love daily, and seek always as many ways as possible to show God's love to others. What you give of God's love will be what you receive back—in multiplied form!

- *What new insights do you have into your identity as a believer in Christ Jesus?*

  _____

  _____

- *In what ways are you feeling challenged in your spirit?*

  _____

  _____

FIVE

REDEEMED

A re you living today knowing fully that you are redeemed?

Do you have the identity of a person who has been freed of sin's bondage?

Do you truly feel fully and forever forgiven?

A good number of Christians today *say* they have been forgiven of all their sins, but they often say this with a small question mark in their voices—they are *hoping* they are forgiven fully rather than *knowing with certainty* that they are forgiven.

Others believe that their sins have been forgiven, but they continue to struggle with sin, and they wonder if their ongoing struggle means that they were not fully forgiven—they have questions about whether they can ever be free of sinful desires and old sinful habits.

The apostle Paul wrote to the Ephesians this wonderful statement about their identity as believers in Christ:

> In Him we have redemption through His blood, the forgiveness of sins, according to the riches of His grace. (Eph. 1:7)

In this lesson we will deal with our true identity as those who have been "redeemed by the blood of Christ Jesus."

- *Have you had experiences that led you to wonder if God had truly forgiven you of your sin nature? Have you had experiences in which you struggled with an ongoing desire to sin?*

- *How do you feel when you hear the statement, "as a believer you are redeemed and forgiven"?*

Forgiveness of Our Sins

Paul uses two words in describing the believer's relationship to sin: *redemption* and *forgiveness*. We'll deal with the latter of these two terms first since it is the term with which most of us are more familiar.

To be forgiven is to be set free from any guilt and any consequences over one's past sins. It is to have the "sin slate" of one's life totally wiped clean.

Sin is regarded throughout the Bible as a state of bondage that is the result of transgressions, iniquity, and evil. We commit sin because we *are* sinners. We were born with a sin nature. Our sinful actions further seal the fact that we are sinners. Our being and doing are cyclical.

Every sinner knows—at some level, intuitive or conscious— that he or she is sinning. Sin involves the will, and because it involves the will, it involves our memory. We remember our sins. They don't just float by unnoticed or ignored. The psalmist acknowledged this in writing, "For I acknowledge my transgressions, / And my sin is always before me" (Ps. 51:3).

Because each of us is born with a sin nature and commits sin, each of us is in need of forgiveness. There is no person who is naturally good or without sin. Every person is in need of God's salvation so that we do not experience the spiritual consequences of sin.

Before . . .

Our state prior to our receiving God's forgiveness is this: we were living in sin, the end result of which is eternal death. God's nature is holiness and truth, and He cannot abide where evil and unrighteousness are allowed to reign. (God loves the sinner always, but He is never content to allow a sinner to continue in sin because as long as the person continues in sin, he is just beyond the reach of God's forgiveness. God is always seeking to bring a sinner to a decision to receive the forgiveness offered through Jesus Christ so that He might cause a spiritual rebirth in that person and abide with him.)

After . . .

Our state *after* receiving God's forgiveness is this: we are living in the righteousness of Jesus Christ, and we are the inheritors of eternal life. By the power of His Holy Spirit, God abides within us and lives out His life through us.

Every believer is a walking picture of "before and after." Before Christ, we were unforgiven and were on a path to eternal death. In Christ, we are forgiven and are on a path toward eternal life.

What the Word Says	What the Word Says to Me
For all have sinned and fall short of the glory of God. (Rom. 3:23)	....
If we say that we have no sin, we deceive ourselves, and the truth is not in us . . . If we say that we have not sinned, we make Him a liar, and His word is not in us. (1 John 1:8, 10)	....
For the wages of sin is death, but the gift of God is eternal life in Christ Jesus our Lord. (Rom. 6:23)	....

And you He made alive, who were dead in trespasses and sins. (Eph. 2:1)

And you, being dead in your trespasses and the uncircumcision of your flesh, He has made alive together with Him, having forgiven you all trespasses. (Col. 2:13)

Total Forgiveness

So many people seem to think that the slate of their trespasses and sins has been only partially wiped clean. They look at the gravity and the nature of their sin and wonder, "Could God ever fully forgive *that type of sin?*" Others look at the great number of their sins and question, "Could God ever fully forgive *so much sin?*" Still others look at the magnitude of a particular sin and ask, "Could God ever fully forgive *such a great sin?*" The answer to each question is an unqualified yes!

In the first place, God does not place qualifiers or adjectives on sin. No one type of sin is any greater or lesser, blacker or darker, than any other kind of sin. Before God, sin is sin. Neither does God look at the amount of sin in a person's life and declare that with the addition of one more sin, a person moves from a "forgivable" to an "unforgivable" column. All sin, no matter the amount, is equal before God—one sin is the same as one million sins, one type of sin is just as consequential as any other.

In the second place, when God forgives sin, He forgives it completely, even to the point of *forgetting it entirely!* Not one shred of sin is left over for later forgiveness. God's ability to forgive sin is infinite and inexhaustible.

What the Word Says	What the Word Says to Me
Bless the LORD, O my soul,	
And forget not all His benefits:	
Who forgives all your	
iniquities . . .	
Who redeems your life from	
destruction,	
Who crowns you with loving-	
kindness and tender mercies.	
(Ps. 103:2–4)	
For as the heavens are high	
above the earth,	
So great is His mercy toward	
those who fear Him;	
As far as the east is from the	
west,	
So far has He removed our	
transgressions from us.	
(Ps. 103:11–12)	
You have lovingly delivered	
my soul from the pit of	
corruption,	
For You have cast all my sins	
behind Your back. (Isa. 38:17)	

No One Who Seeks God's Forgiveness Is Turned Away

One of the awesome aspects of God's character is that He is merciful and forgiving to all who seek His forgiveness. All who ask God for forgiveness are granted it. Jesus said, "The one who comes to Me I will by no means cast out" (John 6:37).

Our part is to come to God with a humble heart and to confess the fact that we have sinned and are in need of forgiveness, to accept Jesus Christ's sacrifice on the cross as being for us personally, and to receive the forgiveness God offers. God's response to our confession is always to forgive.

There simply is no basis for *not* accepting God's forgiveness—it is freely offered to all, costs us personally nothing to receive, and results in the guaranteed benefits of freedom from guilt and eternal life!

What the Word Says

If we confess our sins, He is faithful and just to forgive us our sins and to cleanse us from all unrighteousness. (1 John 1:9)

"Come now, and let us reason together,"
Says the LORD,
"Though your sins are like scarlet,
They shall be as white as snow;
Though they are red like crimson,
They shall be as wool." (Isa. 1:18)

Repent therefore and be converted, that your sins may be blotted out, so that times of refreshing may come from the presence of the Lord. (Acts 3:19)

What the Word Says to Me

• *Have you had an experience of confessing your sins and receiving God's forgiveness?*

_____

_____

Our Lingering Guilt

Many people experience God's forgiveness but then suffer from lingering guilt over their past sins. To continue to hang on to guilt after receiving God's forgiveness is to say to God, "Your forgiveness wasn't enough." And surely it is!

The challenge for many of us is to *accept* God's total forgiveness and then to forgive ourselves and to move forward in our lives. To hang on to guilt and shame is to devalue what Christ Jesus did on the cross.

What the Word Says	What the Word Says to Me
There is therefore now no condemnation to those who are in Christ Jesus. (Rom. 8:1)	....
Therefore if the Son makes you free, you shall be free indeed. (John 8:36)	....

• *In what ways are you feeling challenged in your spirit today?*

_____

_____

• *What new insights do you have into your identity as a person who has been forgiven of all sin and set free from all guilt and shame?*

_____

_____

Redeemed from Being a Slave to Sin

Not only are you forgiven, but you have been redeemed from sin's bondage.

To be redeemed is to be "delivered by payment of debt." Redemption is the *purchase* of something that has a debt against it. We see this in the way pawnshops are operated: those who buy things at pawnshops are buying items that have a debt against them. As we discussed earlier in this lesson, sinners carry a "debt" of sin. In their sinful state, they are living under a death sentence.

When Christ died on the cross, He paid our sin debt and purchased us for God.

The apostle Paul likened our purchase to the slave markets of the Roman Empire. He wrote,

> Do you not know that to whom you present yourselves slaves to obey, you are that one's slaves whom you obey, whether of sin leading to death, or of obedience leading to righteousness? But God be thanked that though you were slaves of sin, yet you obeyed from the heart . . . And having been set free from sin, you became slaves of righteousness . . . Now having been set free from sin, and having become slaves of God, you have your fruit to holiness, and the end, everlasting life. (Rom. 6:16–18, 22)

Slaves do what they are compelled to do by their masters. Paul stated that those who are still in a sinful state are slaves to their sin nature. They behave as they do because their sin nature compels them to do what is unrighteous in God's eyes.

Those who have received God's forgiveness, however, have the Holy Spirit dwelling within them, and they are compelled to act in a righteous way because of His presence.

> • *Can you recall an experience you had when you were a sinner in which you sinned almost "in spite of yourself"—when*

you felt compelled to sin even though you knew what you were doing was wrong before God?

Only a free person can buy a slave, and the only truly "free" person who ever walked this earth from birth was Christ Jesus. He was the only One capable of purchasing us off the "slave market of sin." By His shed blood, He made it possible not only for us to be forgiven, but for us to be redeemed *so that we no longer have a sin nature and we no longer are slaves to sin.*

What does this mean? It means that we as believers in Christ Jesus do not *have* to sin. The Holy Spirit dwelling in us will do His utmost to guide us to keep us from sinning, and if we sin, the Holy Spirit will convict us so that we will confess our sin and repent of it! To sin is no longer our natural impulse. Sin has become unnatural and abhorrent to us. Our redemption means that we are now in the process of losing all desire to sin. John wrote,

> If anyone sins, we have an Advocate with the Father, Jesus Christ the righteous . . . Now by this we know that we know Him, if we keep His commandments. He who says, "I know Him," and does not keep His commandments, is a liar, and the truth is not in him. But whoever keeps His word, truly the love of God is perfected in him. By this we know that we are in Him. He who says he abides in Him ought himself also to walk just as He walked. (1 John 2:1, 3–6)

• *How do you feel knowing that you are redeemed from the very impulse to commit sin?*

Can We Really Live Any Way We Want to Live?

Many people question the security of salvation, falsely believing that a Christian can be saved and then live any way he or she chooses, without consequence. Friend, there is always consequence to sin! The believer in Christ Jesus may not lose his salvation and eternal life if he chooses to sin, but he is setting himself up for a lifetime of misery if he sins in the face of God's loving forgiveness. The Holy Spirit acts within the believer to convict the believer of sin and to draw the believer immediately back to the throne of God, to confess that sin and to receive forgiveness for it. The person who willfully and repeatedly chooses to pursue a life of sin is very likely not a person who has truly been born again. As John wrote,

> Whoever believes that Jesus is the Christ is born of God, and everyone who loves Him who begot also loves him who is begotten of Him. By this we know that we love the children of God, when we love God and keep His commandments. For this is the love of God, that we keep His commandments. And His commandments are not burdensome. For whatever is born of God overcomes the world. And this is the victory that has overcome the world—our faith. (1 John 5:1–4)

The person who truly has been redeemed and forgiven of his sins is a person who will no longer have a desire or an automatic impulse to sin. Rather, the very *nature* of the person has been changed so their desire is for the things of God.

- *What new insights do you have into what it means to be redeemed?*

_____

_____

What the Word Says	**What the Word Says to Me**
For the death that He died, He died to sin once for all; but the life that He lives, He lives to God. Likewise you also, reckon yourselves to be dead indeed to sin, but alive to God in Christ Jesus our Lord. (Rom. 6:10–11)	....
You were not redeemed with corruptible things, like silver or gold, from your aimless conduct received by tradition from your fathers, but with the precious blood of Christ, as of a lamb without blemish and without spot. (1 Peter 1:18–19)	....
He has delivered us from the power of darkness and translated us into the kingdom of the Son of His love, in whom we have redemption through His blood, the forgiveness of sins. (Col. 1:13–14)	....

Living with a Forgiven Identity

Those who have been forgiven are called to do three things: to forgive others, to share God's message of forgiveness with others, and to walk as forgiven saints in Christ Jesus.

To forgive others is a commandment. Jesus said,

- "Be merciful, just as your Father also is merciful. Judge not, and you shall not be judged. Condemn not, and you shall not be condemned. Forgive, and you will be forgiven." (Luke 6:36–37)
- "And whenever you stand praying, if you have anything against anyone, forgive him, that your Father in heaven may also forgive you your trespasses. But if you do not forgive, neither will your Father in heaven forgive your trespasses." (Mark 11:25–26)
- "Then his master, after he had called him, said to him, 'You wicked servant! I forgave you all that debt because you begged me. Should you not also have had compassion on your fellow servant, just as I had pity on you?' And his master was angry, and delivered him to the torturers until he should pay all that was due to him. So My heavenly Father also will do to you if each of you, from his heart, does not forgive his brother his trespasses." (Matt. 18:32–35)

The salvation and forgiveness we have received freely from the Lord we are to give freely to others (see Matt. 10:8).

- *In what ways are you feeling challenged in your spirit?*

_____

_____

Proclaiming God's Forgiveness

We are never to keep the good news of God's forgiveness to ourselves—rather, we are to use every opportunity given to us to tell others about God's love and offer of salvation. In forgiving others, we give witness of God's desire to forgive. But we must go beyond the example of our lives to actually telling others that God loves them and *how* they can receive God's forgiveness by believing in Jesus Christ and accepting His death on the cross as the one definitive sacrifice for sin.

What the Word Says	**What the Word Says to Me**
And if anyone sins, we have an Advocate with the Father, Jesus Christ the righteous. And He Himself is the propitiation for our sins, and not for ours only but also for the whole world. (1 John 2:1–2)	....
And this is the testimony: that God has given us eternal life, and this life is in His Son. He who has the Son has life; he who does not have the Son of God does not have life. (1 John 5:11–12)	....
[Jesus said,] "Go into all the world and preach the gospel to every creature. He who believes and is baptized will be saved; but he who does not believe will be condemned." (Mark 16:15–16)	....

Living in Repentance

Finally, we are to live as forgiven saints, walking boldly into the life that God has for us. This means true repentance—turning from all things that we know are displeasing to God and choosing to obey His commandments. Our identity is no longer associated with darkness, evil, guilt, shame, or death. Rather, our identity is linked to light, goodness, love, joy, and eternal life! We are to walk truly as children of the light! (See 1 John 1:7.)

What the Word Says

Therefore submit to God.
Resist the devil and he will flee
from you. Draw near to God
and He will draw near to you.
Cleanse your hands, you sinners; and purify your hearts,
you double-minded . . . Humble yourselves in the sight of
the Lord, and He will lift you
up. (James 4:7–8, 10)

If we say that we have fellowship with Him, and walk in
darkness, we lie and do not
practice the truth. But if we
walk in the light as He is in the
light, we have fellowship with
one another, and the blood of
Jesus Christ His Son cleanses
us from all sin. (1 John 1:6–7)

We give thanks to the God and
Father of our Lord Jesus
Christ, praying always for you,
since we heard of your faith in
Christ Jesus . . . For this reason
we also, since the day we heard
it, do not cease to pray for you,
and to ask that you may be
filled with the knowledge of
His will in all wisdom and spiritual understanding; that you
may walk worthy of the Lord,

What the Word Says to Me

fully pleasing Him, being fruitful in every good work and
increasing in the knowledge of
God. (Col. 1:3–4, 9–10)

- *What new insights do you have into your identity as a for-given saint in Christ Jesus?*

- *In what ways are you feeling challenged in your spirit?*

SIX

HEIR

Are you aware that you are the recipient of a grand inheritance?

So many people daydream at some point in their lives of receiving an unexpected inheritance from a wealthy person. The fact is, as a believer in Christ Jesus, you *are* the heir of the most incredible, awesome, lavish inheritance any person could ever dream to receive!

Paul wrote to the Ephesians, "In Him also we have obtained an inheritance" (Eph. 1:11). And what is that inheritance? Paul described it in these terms in the epistle to the Ephesians and elsewhere:

- "blessed us with every spiritual blessing in the heavenly places in Christ" (Eph. 1:3)
- "exceeding riches of His grace" (Eph. 2:7)
- "treasure in earthen vessels" (2 Cor. 4:7)
- "riches of His glory" (Eph. 3:16)

Paul declared, "Eye has not seen, nor ear heard, / Nor have entered into the heart of man / The things which God has prepared for those who love Him" (1 Cor. 2:9). The inheritance we have in Christ Jesus is so glorious, so vast, and so tremendous that we cannot even comprehend it with our finite minds. As Paul wrote to the Ephesians, "Now to Him who is able to do *exceedingly abundantly above all that we ask or think,* according to the power that works in us, to Him be glory in the church by Christ Jesus to all generations, forever and ever. Amen" (Eph. 3:20–21, emphasis mine).

The inheritance God has prepared for us as believers in Christ Jesus is an overflowing, abundant inheritance. Nothing of benefit or goodness has been withheld from us.

- *How do you feel when you think of yourself as being the recipient of God's great inheritance?*

_____

_____

What the Word Says	What the Word Says to Me
The Spirit Himself bears witness with our spirit that we are children of God, and if children, then heirs—heirs of God and joint heirs with Christ. (Rom. 8:16–17)	....
Because you are sons, God has sent forth the Spirit of His Son into your hearts, crying out, "Abba, Father!" Therefore you are no longer a slave but a son, and if a son, then an heir of God through Christ. (Gal. 4:6–7)	....

Rich or Poor?

Many Christians see themselves as being poor. Some have this identity because they have been taught incorrectly that Christians are to be poor and uneducated. There is no justification in Scripture for a Christian to be either poor or ignorant. To the contrary, Paul declared to the Philippians, "My God shall supply all your need according to His riches in glory by Christ Jesus" (Phil. 4:19). We are to study and know the truth of God's Word and to be well-informed about our inheritance.

Rich or poor is never a matter of one's bank account or investment portfolio. "Rich" and "poor" are first and foremost a state of the heart—we respond to life with generosity or stinginess, with fear or boldness, based to a great extent on how rich we believe ourselves to be in Christ Jesus and to the extent that we are trusting God to supply all of our needs, now and every day in the future.

Our identity as believers must always be based upon what we know to be true in God's Word, not on how we feel or what others say about us. We must never draw our identity from unbelievers. The sad fact, however, is that many Christians are looking to the world for their identity, and they are coming up with a conclusion that they are poor or lacking in some way.

The world always bases its conclusions upon *comparison*, and if you compare yourself to others, you will lose on every point every time. Why? Because you can always find *somebody* who has more, does more, is endowed with more, possesses more, or achieves more than you do in any given area of life. Even if you are the world record holder today in a particular field, you are not likely to be the world record holder ten years from now!

God never calls us to compare ourselves to others. He calls us to look to Christ Jesus, and He says to us, "You are in Christ. There is no comparison to those who are in Christ. You have it *all*—not only now, but forever. Anything of lasting value or benefit, anything of great worth or worthiness, I have given you in Christ Jesus. You have all of Him, and He has all of anything that truly matters!"

- *Have you ever had an experience in which you felt worthless by comparison to another person?*

- *Have you had experiences in which you felt "poor"? How did your perception of your own identity impact your feelings about other people? How did it impact your generosity toward others?*

The Nature of Our Inheritance

The Scriptures are very specific about our inheritance in Christ Jesus. Many things are promised to those who are *in Christ*, but in this lesson, we are going to focus on three specific things.

1. We Shall Be Like Christ

In the natural world, adults often look at children and conclude, "He has his father's genes. He is going to look just like his father when he grows up," or "She has her mother's eyes. She's going to be a beauty just like her mom when she's an adult." Physically, we inherit our genes—our physical characteristics and attributes—from our parents.

Spiritually, we each are destined to mature into the very likeness of Christ Jesus. One day we are going to be *like Him*. John wrote,

> Behold what manner of love the Father has bestowed on us, that we should be called children of God! Therefore the world does not know us, because it did not know Him. Beloved, now we are children of God; and it has not yet been revealed what we shall be, but we know that when He is revealed, we shall be like Him, for we shall see Him as He is. (1 John 3:1–2)

Oh, to be like Jesus! To respond to every person and every situation the way Jesus did . . . to live in perfect health and absolute victory every moment of our lives . . . to overcome the enemy of our souls at every turn . . . to have at our disposal all of the power and riches of the Father! That is the inheritance into which we are growing!

Ask yourself, What did Christ desire that Christ did not have? Nothing!

What did Christ want to do that He was incapable of doing? Nothing!

What did Christ long to possess that He could not possess? Nothing!

To be like Christ is to have all that Christ has, to know all that Christ knows, to desire all that Christ desires.

- *What new insights do you have into your identity as a believer in Christ and an heir of God in Christ?*

_____

_____

What the Word Says

For whom He foreknew, He also predestined to be conformed to the image of His Son, that He might be the firstborn among many brethren. (Rom. 8:29)

For our citizenship is in heaven, from which we also eagerly wait for the Savior, the Lord Jesus Christ, who will transform our lowly body that it may be conformed to His glorious body, according to the

What the Word Says to Me

----

working by which He is able
even to subdue all things to
Himself. (Phil. 3:20–21)

······································

······································

······································

2. We Will Reign with Christ

Not only will we be like Christ, but we will also rule with Christ. Paul wrote to the Ephesians that God, in His mercy and because of His great love, had made them alive together with Christ, and then he said that God "raised us up together, and made us sit together in the heavenly places in Christ Jesus" (Eph. 2:6).

Christ is sitting on His throne in heaven today and, in the spiritual realm, as a believer in Christ you are sitting with Him!

Now a young prince who is crowned king may not receive the *fullness* of his authority as king until he reaches majority age; nevertheless, he is the crowned king. The years between the time of his coronation and his assumption of full power are years of growing preparation and increasing authority. This is true for our inheritance to "reign with Christ." We have been crowned "joint heir" with Christ, and, as we mature in Christ Jesus, our authority and understanding and ability to rule and reign increase. The fullness of our ability to rule and reign begins now, but it ends in eternity.

Ask yourself, Was there any force of evil or power of the devil that was beyond the ability of Jesus to rule over it? No!

Was any disease greater than the power of Jesus to heal it? No!

Was any demon in a person more powerful than Jesus' power to cast it out? No!

Was Satan himself more power than Jesus? No!

Christ in us makes us *more than conquerors* (see Rom. 8:37).

What the Word Says

If we endure,
We shall also reign with Him.
(2 Tim. 2:12)

For You were slain,
And have redeemed us to God
by Your blood
Out of every tribe and tongue
and people and nation,
And have made us kings and
priests to our God;
And we shall reign on the
earth. (Rev. 5:9–10)

Therefore God also has highly
exalted Him and given Him
the name which is above every
name, that at the name of
Jesus every knee should bow,
of those in heaven, and of
those on earth, and of those
under the earth, and that every
tongue should confess that
Jesus Christ is Lord, to the
glory of God the Father. (Phil.
2:9–11)

What the Word Says to Me

• *As you look back over your life since you accepted Christ Jesus as your Savior, can you see how the Lord is preparing you to reign with Him?*

3. We'll Have a Heavenly Home with Christ

To have the character and nature of Christ, to rule and reign over all things with Christ—what a great inheritance we have been given! Ultimately, of course, we also have the great inheritance of heaven itself. Jesus said, "I go to prepare a place for you. And if I go and prepare a place for you, I will come again and receive you to Myself; that where I am, there you may be also" (John 14:2–3). To be with Christ forever and ever is our greatest inheritance of all.

Our inherited "family home" is one in which

> "God will wipe away every tear from their eyes; there shall be no more death, nor sorrow, nor crying. There shall be no more pain, for the former things have passed away" . . . And he showed me a pure river of water of life, clear as crystal, proceeding from the throne of God and of the Lamb. In the middle of its street, and on either side of the river, was the tree of life, which bore twelve fruits, each tree yielding its fruit every month. And the leaves of the tree were for the healing of the nations. And there shall be no more curse, but the throne of God and of the Lamb shall be in it, and His servants shall serve Him. They shall see His face, and His name shall be on their foreheads. There shall be no night there: They need no lamp nor light of the sun, for the Lord God gives them light. And they shall reign forever and ever. (Rev. 21:4; 22:1–5)

- *How do you feel when you read about your inheritance as a saint in Christ Jesus?*

  _____

  _____

- *In what ways are you feeling challenged in your spirit?*

  _____

  _____

What the Word Says	**What the Word Says to Me**
Blessed be the God and Father of our Lord Jesus Christ, who according to His abundant mercy has begotten us again to a living hope through the resurrection of Jesus Christ from the dead, to an inheritance incorruptible and undefiled and that does not fade away, reserved in heaven for you, who are kept by the power of God through faith. (1 Peter 1:3–5)	--- --- --- --- --- --- --- --- --- --- --- ---

The Guarantee That We Will Receive Our Full Inheritance

- How can we be assured that we *are* heirs?
- How can we be certain that we will receive the full inheritance that God has for us?

Paul said to the Ephesians, "You were sealed with the Holy Spirit of promise, who is the guarantee of our inheritance until the redemption of the purchased possession, to the praise of His glory" (Eph. 1:13–14). The Holy Spirit dwelling within us is the proof that God has given us a glorious inheritance and that He is going to bring that inheritance to full fruition in us.

Seals in Bible times were used to indicate four things:

1. *Ownership.* Valuable possessions were protected in containers to which a seal of ownership was attached. We are

owned by Christ Jesus, purchased by the price of His shed blood.

2. *Authenticity.* Seals verified that an article was genuine. When the Holy Spirit indwells us, He changes our nature to give authenticity to the truth that Christ Jesus is our Savior and Lord.

3. *Authority.* Official scrolls of kings were sealed to indicate that the documents were backed by the full authority of the king's power and wealth. We are under the authority of God the Father, Son, and Holy Spirit—we are no longer under the authority of the devil.

4. *Completed transactions.* Documents were sealed to indicate that a transaction was complete and established in law. Paul stated repeatedly that we *have* obtained an inheritance in Christ. The transaction of our inheritance was fully completed in Christ's death and resurrection.

What can break what God seals? Nothing.

Who can undo what the Holy Spirit does? No one.

As believers in Christ Jesus, we are sealed forever "according to the good pleasure of His will, to the praise of the glory of His grace" (Eph. 1:5–6).

The work in us that brings us to the point of *receiving* our full inheritance is the work of the Holy Spirit. It is nothing we can achieve or do. It is *His* power that is effective and productive in bringing us to the fullness of Christ's character, authority, and wisdom. It is *His* power that resurrects us to eternal life.

Our part is to trust God, to read God's Word, and to listen to the Holy Spirit's speaking in our hearts to the best of our ability day by day, and to *obey* what we believe God is calling us to do. It is in this way that we will become the person God has designed us to be. It is in this way that we will move into our full inheritance so that it is not only a *potential* inheritance but an *actual* inheritance.

The work in our hearts that prepares us to use our inheritance wisely and for the glory of God is always, however, the work of the Holy Spirit, accomplished in His timing and according to His methods.

What the Word Says	What the Word Says to Me
Now may the God of peace Himself sanctify you completely; and may your whole spirit, soul, and body be preserved blameless at the coming of our Lord Jesus Christ. He who calls you is faithful, who also will do it. (1 Thess. 5:23–24)	....
But the Lord is faithful, who will establish you and guard you from the evil one. (2 Thess. 3:3)	....
Being confident of this very thing, that He who has begun a good work in you will complete it until the day of Jesus Christ. (Phil. 1:6)	....

• *What new insights do you have into your identity as an heir in Christ Jesus?*

_____

_____

• *In what ways are you feeling challenged in your spirit?*

_____

_____

SEVEN

ENLIGHTENED SAINT

Are you aware today that you have been given the mind of Christ?

In order for us to truly reign with Christ and to rule over all things with Him, we must have both the heart and mind of Christ. We must think as He thinks and feel as He feels. We must have both His wisdom and His compassion.

The good news of our inheritance is that in Christ, we have not only inherited the *nature* of Christ—the character traits of His love, joy, peace, patience, goodness, kindness, faithfulness, gentleness, and self-control—but we have been given Christ's ability to make wise decisions and sound judgments.

Paul wrote to the Ephesians that the riches of God's grace abound toward us "in all wisdom and prudence" (Eph. 1:8). He said that God has "made known to us the mystery of His will" and given us "the spirit of wisdom and revelation in the knowledge of Him" (Eph. 1:9; 1:17). Paul's prayer for the Ephesians was that the eyes of their understanding might be "enlightened; that you may know what is the hope of His calling, what are the riches of the glory of His inheritance in the saints, and what is the exceeding greatness of His power toward us who believe" (Eph. 1:18–19).

Ask yourself, What did Christ want to know that He was incapable of knowing? Nothing!

What did Christ desire to understand that He could not understand? Nothing!

What remained a mystery to Christ about God the Father? Nothing!

Just as a child grows in his ability to *use* all of the brain cells that he is given at birth, so we grow in our ability to understand the deeper things of God *as we grow in our relationship with Christ Jesus.* Our inheritance is to have the *mind* of Christ!

What the Word Says	What the Word Says to Me
Let this mind be in you which was also in Christ Jesus. (Phil. 2:5)	....
Now we have received, not the spirit of the world, but the Spirit who is from God, that we might know the things that have been freely given to us by God. These things we also speak, not in words which man's wisdom teaches but which the Holy Spirit teaches, comparing spiritual things with spiritual. But the natural man does not receive the things of the Spirit of God, for they are foolishness to him; nor can he know them, because they are spiritually discerned . . . But we have the mind of Christ. (1 Cor. 2:12–14, 16)	....

If any of you lacks wisdom, let
him ask of God, who gives to
all liberally and without
reproach, and it will be given
to him. But let him ask in
faith, with no doubting. (James
1:5–6)

....
....
....
....
....
....
....

Do not be conformed to this
world, but be transformed by
the renewing of your mind,
that you may prove what is
that good and acceptable and
perfect will of God. (Rom.
12:2)

....
....
....
....
....
....

> • *Prior to your acceptance of Christ Jesus as your Savior, did
> you have experiences in which you read but did not under-
> stand the Word of God? Have you had experiences since your
> acceptance of Christ in which you realized that you now
> understand the Bible more clearly and more fully?*

_____

_____

Three Things We Are to Know

Paul identified three things the believer in Christ is to know
with an "overflowing understanding"—the hope of His calling,
the riches of the glory of Christ's inheritance in the saints, and
the exceeding greatness of Christ's power. In this lesson we are
going to look at each of these areas in which we are privileged
to experience "enlightenment."

1. The Hope of His Calling on Our Lives

So many people say as an excuse for failing to become
involved in ministry outreaches, "God doesn't have a calling

on my life" or more specifically, "I'm not called to be a minister." Most of these people have an erroneous understanding that only those who are in full-time ministry service are "called." The fact is, we each are called of God to be ministers, people who attempt to meet the spiritual, emotional, and physical needs of others. To minister is to pray, to listen, to give wise counsel, to give a witness to the gospel, to tell what we know about God's Word, to love, to bless, to share one's resources, to affirm, to exercise our ministry gifts given to us by the Holy Spirit. We each are called to do this!

The Bible gives us three descriptions about our call from God as saints.

1. *An upward call.* Paul wrote to the Philippians, "Brethren, I do not count myself to have apprehended; but one thing I do, forgetting those things which are behind and reaching forward to those things which are ahead, I press toward the goal for the prize of the *upward call* of God in Christ Jesus" (Phil. 3:13–14, emphasis mine).

God's call on our lives is a call that continually compels us to reach for higher moral standards, higher levels of understanding, higher character traits, higher ethical conduct, higher degrees of spiritual perfection. We are called to grow, develop, and mature in Christ Jesus so that we might be genuine, godly servants. God calls us to be the best we can be.

2. *A holy calling.* Paul wrote to Timothy, "Share with me in the sufferings for the gospel according to the power of God, who has saved us and called us with a *holy calling,* not according to our works, but according to His own purpose and grace which was given to us in Christ Jesus before time began" (2 Tim. 1:8–9, emphasis mine).

To be holy is to be separated for use by God. It is to be refined and cleansed so that we no longer think like the world or pursue the lusts of the flesh, the lusts of the eyes, or the pride of life. It is to see ourselves as agents of righteousness, infusing the world with God's purpose and God's goodness as "salt" that preserves, heals, and gives zest to life.

Our calling is a call to serve God by serving others.

3. *A heavenly calling.* Our calling is always to live a godly life that will influence others to accept Christ and receive eternal life. Everything we do as believers in Christ Jesus should be done so that it might bear spiritual fruit and have eternal benefit. In Hebrews 3:1 we read, "Therefore, holy brethren, partakers of the *heavenly calling,* consider the Apostle and High Priest of our confession, Christ Jesus" (emphasis mine). We are no longer citizens of this world, but rather we are citizens of heaven—our purpose being to pray that God's will *will* be done on this earth as it is in heaven, and to obey the leading of the Holy Spirit so that we might have a part in making God's will a reality on earth.

- *What new insights do you have into your calling as a believer in Christ?*

_____

_____

What the Word Says

For this reason we also, since the day we heard it, do not cease to pray for you, and to ask that you may be filled with the knowledge of His will in all wisdom and spiritual understanding; that you may walk worthy of the Lord, fully pleasing Him, being fruitful in every good work and increasing in the knowledge of God; strengthened with all might, according to His glorious power, for all patience and longsuffering with joy; giving

What the Word Says to Me

_____

_____

_____

_____

_____

_____

_____

_____

_____

_____

_____

_____

_____

thanks to the Father who has
qualified us to be partakers of
the inheritance of the saints in
the light. (Col. 1:9–12)

Our Father in heaven,
Hallowed be Your name.
Your kingdom come.
Your will be done
On earth as it is in heaven.
(Matt. 6:9–10)

• *How do you feel about being called of God?*

_____

_____

2. The Riches of the Glory of His Inheritance in the Saints

God not only desires that we know our *calling* in Christ, but that we have an overflowing understanding about who we *are* from God's perspective. Paul wrote to the Ephesians that he longed for them to be enlightened about the "riches of the glory of His inheritance in the saints" (Eph. 1:18).

Whose inheritance? Christ's inheritance!

God gives us all that Christ is, has, and does—His nature, His reign, His eternal life. But what does God give to Christ Jesus as *His* inheritance? Us!

God says to Jesus Christ, in effect, "Look what a wonderful inheritance I have for You. I have Joe and Roger and Billy for You. I have Sue and Marilyn and Katherine for You."

So many Christians seem to have the attitude, "Well, I'm saved and that's enough." No! You are the inheritance of Christ Jesus. Don't you long to be all that you can be for *His* sake? Don't you desire to present yourself holy, an unblemished and spotless bride? Don't you desire to leave behind all of the "old you" that was in full force before you accepted Christ and to become all that the "new you" can possibly be?

When we truly catch a glimpse of how God regards us—the rich inheritance of Christ Jesus—we will not only place a much higher value upon ourselves, but upon all those who are saints with us in Christ Jesus.

What the Word Says	What the Word Says to Me
I will greatly rejoice in the LORD, My soul shall be joyful in my God; For He has clothed me with the garments of salvation, He has covered me with the robe of righteousness, As a bridegroom decks himself with ornaments, And as a bride adorns herself with her jewels. For as the earth brings forth its bud, As the garden causes the things that are sown in it to spring forth, So the Lord GOD will cause righteousness and praise to spring forth before all the nations. (Isa. 61:10–11)	....
[Jesus said,] "Blessed are those who hunger and thirst for righteousness, for they shall be filled." (Matt. 5:6)	....

• *How do you feel about being Christ's inheritance?*

_____

_____

• *In what ways are you feeling challenged in your spirit?*

_____

_____

3. The Greatness of His Power in Us

No believer ever has justification for saying, "I'm a weakling." As believers in Christ, we have the omnipotent power of God residing in us! Paul wrote to the Ephesians that he desired for them to know this:

> the exceeding greatness of His power toward us who believe, according to the working of His mighty power which He worked in Christ when He raised Him from the dead and seated Him at His right hand in the heavenly places, far above all principality and power and might and dominion, and every name that is named, not only in this age but also in that which is to come.
>
> And He put all things under His feet, and gave Him to be head over all things to the church, which is His body, the fullness of Him who fills all in all. (Eph. 1:19–23)

There is no power greater than that of the Lord who lives in us. The words that Paul used for power reflect energy, strength, and might. The power of the Holy Spirit in us is:

• *Resurrection power.* The same power that raised Christ from the dead now resides in you.
• *Power over all spiritual darkness.* The power within us is greater than that of any force of evil.
• *Power over all the systems of the world—whether they are*

natural, spiritual, or human in origin. All things have been put under the feet of Christ.

Just as a little child grows up into the full use of his own phsyical strength and ability, so we are growing up in our spiritual strength and power in Christ Jesus. Even as we do, we must recognize at all times that the Holy Spirit in us is *greater* than any other form of power we can ever experience and that God in us is greater than anything that comes against us (see 1 John 4:4).

How do we activate the power of God in our lives? By waiting on the Lord in quiet trust and by praising God. Waiting upon the Lord brings us to a greater realization of all that He has done for us and all that He is. Praise releases joy into our hearts, and the joy of the Lord *is* our strength.

What the Word Says	What the Word Says to Me
[Jesus said,] "You shall receive power when the Holy Spirit has come upon you; and you shall be witnesses to Me in Jerusalem, and in all Judea and Samaria, and to the end of the earth." (Acts 1:8)	....
He who is in you is greater than he who is in the world. (1 John 4:4)	....
His divine power has given to us all things that pertain to life and godliness, through the knowledge of Him who called us. (2 Peter 1:3)	....
The LORD is my rock and my	....

fortress and my deliverer;
My God, my strength, in
whom I will trust;
My shield and the horn of my
salvation, my stronghold.
I will call upon the LORD, who
is worthy to be praised;
So shall I be saved from my
enemies. (Ps. 18:2–3)

The joy of the LORD is your
strength. (Neh. 8:10)

- *How do you feel about being the recipient of God's "exceeding" power?*

_____

_____

To Know Christ

While we are to know our calling, who we are in Christ, and the power of the Holy Spirit in us, the greatest "knowing" we can ever have is "knowing Christ."

This does not mean knowing *about* Christ, but knowing Christ. The more we know Christ, the more we know what He desires for us to do in each and every circumstance we face. In that, we know our calling.

The more we know Christ and develop an ever-deepening, intimate relationship with Him, the more we value who He is transforming us to be. In that, we know the richness of our own identity.

The more we know Christ and rely upon Him for daily strength and energy, the more we know His power in us.

Knowing Christ is the key—not merely knowing *about* Him.

What the Word Says	What the Word Says to Me
For this reason I also suffer these things; nevertheless I am not ashamed, for I know whom I have believed. (2 Tim. 1:12)	....
And we know that the Son of God has come and has given us an understanding, that we may know Him who is true; and we are in Him who is true, in His Son Jesus Christ. (1 John 5:20)	....

Our Response to Being Enlightened

Why do we need to know that we are called of God? So that we will have hope about our own future and have a direction for our lives.

Why do we need to know that we are the inheritance of Christ Jesus? So that we will begin to reflect the value that God places upon us.

Why do we need to know that we have been given exceedingly great power in the Holy Spirit? So we will act boldly and be courageous in the face of evil, doubt, and persecution.

The good news is not only that we *must* be enlightened about our position in Christ Jesus, but that we *are* given this wisdom and revelation. God has given us the ability to know, the ability to understand, the ability to discern, the ability to make sound judgments and wise decisions.

The things of God are not a mystery to the believer—to the unbeliever, yes, but not to the believer. God desires for you to have all the information you need to live an effective, successful, godly life. He does not play a guess-if-you-can game with

His children. He imparts to us the wisdom we need, the power we need, and the esteem we need.

Our part is to read and study God's Word. Our part is to come to God in prayer and to seek a daily, abiding relationship with Him.

God's part is to quicken His Word to our Spirit and to increase our knowledge and understanding. His part is to lead and to guide us into the paths of righteousness.

As you read through the Scriptures below, make each one a prayer for yourself. Claim by your faith that you truly are an enlightened saint of God!

What the Word Says	What the Word Says to Me
For God has not given us a spirit of fear, but of power and of love and of a sound mind. (2 Tim. 1:7)	....
[Jesus said,] "When He, the Spirit of truth, has come, He will guide you into all truth; for He will not speak on His own authority, but whatever He hears He will speak; and He will tell you things to come. He will glorify Me, for He will take of what is Mine and declare it to you." (John 16:13–14)	....
You, through Your commandments, make me wiser than my enemies . . . I have more understanding than all my teachers,	....

For Your testimonies are my
meditation.
I understand more than the
ancients,
Because I keep Your
precepts . . .
Through Your precepts I get
understanding;
Therefore I hate every false
way.
Your word is a lamp to my feet
And a light to my path.
(Ps. 119:98–100, 104–5)

- *What new insights do you have into your identity as a believer in Christ Jesus?*

- *In what ways are you feeling challenged in your spirit?*

EIGHT

MEMBER OF THE BODY

Do you ever question if you really "fit" anywhere? Do you have a firm understanding that you belong—that you are a full member of Christ's body?

Paul wrote to the Ephesians that the church—which is composed of all true believers in Christ Jesus—is "His body, the fullness of Him who fills all in all" (Eph. 1:23).

Prior to being a part of the body of Christ, you were an individual—alone and isolated. You were not able to enter into a relationship with God, and, therefore, you were not capable of having an eternal, fully reconciled relationship with another human being.

"But," you may say, "people who aren't in Christ fall in love, get married, have children, make friends, and are in relationship with other people." Yes—but only at a surface level. Without genuine forgiveness and love, no person can truly enter into an abiding, eternal, deep relationship with another person. Our ability to give forgiveness and to express love is always drawn ultimately from our having received forgiveness and love from God. The believer alone is the person who experiences such forgiveness and love.

Those who are separate from Christ are separate from God and from other believers.

Those who are in Christ are no longer separated from God or other believers—rather, they are united together as *one body.*

Paul described this reconciliation with other believers in his letter to the Ephesians, saying,

> Therefore remember that you, once Gentiles in the flesh—who are called Uncircumcision by what is called the Circumcision made in the flesh by hands—that at that time you were without Christ, being aliens from the commonwealth of Israel and strangers from the covenants of promise, having no hope and without God in the world. But now in Christ Jesus you who once were far off have been brought near by the blood of Christ. (Eph. 2:11–13)

To be "brought near" by the blood of Christ means to enter into an intimate relationship with God and to be fully "accepted in the Beloved" as Paul wrote earlier in his epistle. (See Eph. 1:6.) To be "brought near" is also a Jewish term relating to the Temple.

The courts of the temple were arranged so that the "court of the Gentiles" was the farthest court from the Holy of Holies, which held the ark of the covenant and which was the seat of God's presence among the Israelites. The next court closest to the Holy of Holies was the court of the righteous Jewish women. The next court was the court of the righteous Jewish men. The inner court was reserved for those who served as priests before God.

In Christ, believers are brought into the very presence of God—regardless of whether they were originally Jews or Gentiles. Belief in Christ Jesus brings us into the direct presence of God Almighty.

Furthermore, Jesus taught that we, as believers in Him, are united completely with Him and with the Father. He prayed for us the night He prayed for His disciples:

I do not pray for these alone, but also for those who will believe in Me through their word; that they all may be one, as You, Father, are in Me, and I in You; that they also may be one in Us, that the world may believe that You sent me. And the glory which You gave Me I have given them, that they may be one just as We are one: I in them, and You in Me; that they may be made perfect in one, and that the world may know that You have sent Me, and have loved them as You have loved Me. (John 17:20–23)

- *What new insights do you have into your identity as a member of the body of Christ?*

_____

_____

What the Word Says

For as we have many members in one body, but all the members do not have the same function, so we, being many, are one body in Christ, and individually members of one another. (Rom. 12:4–5)

The bread which we break, is it not the communion of the body of Christ? For we, though many, are one bread and one body; for we all partake of that one bread. (1 Cor. 10:16–17)

For by one Spirit we were all baptized into one body— whether Jews or Greeks,

What the Word Says to Me

----

whether slaves or free—and
have all been made to drink
into one Spirit. (1 Cor. 12:13)

Peace Within the Body

The key word that Paul used in describing our new identity of belonging to the body of Christ was *peace*. He said,

> For He Himself is our peace, who has made both one, and has broken down the middle wall of separation, having abolished in His flesh the enmity, that is, the law of commandments contained in ordinances, so as to create in Himself one new man from the two, thus making peace, and that He might reconcile them both to God in one body through the cross, thereby putting to death the enmity. And He came and preached peace to you who were afar off and to those who were near. For through Him we both have access by one Spirit to the Father.
>
> Now, therefore, you are no longer strangers and foreigners, but fellow citizens with the saints and members of the household of God. (Eph. 2:14–19)

Our ability to be at peace with other people flows from Christ, who abides in us as Peacemaker. No law can ever truly unite two people to be at peace with each other. No "peace treaty" can ever bring about lasting peace unless all parties involved have peace in their hearts regarding one another.

Again and again on the world stage, we see peace treaties erupt into open war. Why? Because what was drafted on paper had not been written first on the hearts of the people. Again and again we find individuals claiming they are at "peace" with each other, only to see that peace shattered by arguments and hostile attitudes. Why? Because the peace they claimed was only on the surface—it was not a true peace in their hearts.

Christ alone makes lasting and genuine peace possible.

It is when we recognize and accept Christ's peace within that we can enter into a ministry of reconciliation with others. A ministry of reconciliation means that we become peacemakers ourselves—speaking God's peace to those who are sinners and inviting them to enter a reconciled relationship with God. We also speak peace to our fellow believers, that we all might become fully united in the Spirit.

What the Word Says	What the Word Says to Me
Now all things are of God, who has reconciled us to Himself through Jesus Christ, and has given us the ministry of reconciliation, that is, that God was in Christ reconciling the world to Himself, not imputing their trespasses to them, and has committed to us the word of reconciliation. Now then we are ambassadors for Christ, as though God were pleading through us: we implore you on Christ's behalf, be reconciled to God. (2 Cor. 5:18–20)	
Blessed are the peacemakers, For they shall be called sons of God. (Matt. 5:9)	
Let the peace of God rule in your hearts, to which also you were called in one body. (Col. 3:15)	
For the kingdom of God is . . .	

righteousness and peace and
joy in the Holy Spirit. For he
who serves Christ in these
things is acceptable to God
and approved by men. Therefore let us pursue the things
which make for peace and the
things by which one may edify
another. (Rom. 14:17–19)

God has called us to peace.
(1 Cor. 7:15)

I, therefore, the prisoner of the
Lord, beseech you to walk
worthy of the calling with
which you were called, with all
lowliness and gentleness, with
longsuffering, bearing with one
another in love, endeavoring to
keep the unity of the Spirit in
the bond of peace.
(Eph. 4:1–3)

- *Have you had an experience in which the Lord has reconciled you to others with whom you were estranged prior to
  your acceptance of Christ? Have you had an experience in
  which you felt genuine peace and love in your heart toward
  a person you previously did not like?*

We Are God's Temple

One of the great illustrations that Paul used to describe the body of Christ was that of a temple. He wrote to the Ephesians that they were members of the

> household of God, having been built on the foundation of the apostles and prophets, Jesus Christ Himself being the chief cornerstone, in whom the whole building, being joined together, grows into a holy temple in the Lord, in whom you also are being built together for a dwelling place of God in the Spirit. (Eph. 2:19–22)

Paul was writing to people who were living in the shadow of a great temple to the pagan goddess Diana—the temple was one of the seven wonders of the ancient world. This temple, like all temples to pagan gods, was built to bring "glory" to the goddess Diana. The Greeks held to the opinion that the god or goddess that had the greatest temple was the god or goddess with the most importance—and of course, the thinking went that the most important god or goddess would surely reside in the most important city on earth. The Ephesians claimed that place of preeminence for themselves because of the temple they had built to their goddess.

Paul used this understanding as a springboard for a deeper teaching about the identity of the believer. He said, "You are a holy temple in the Lord." He saw the believers as a dwelling place of God in the spirit—a magnificent temple that was not made with human hands but that was created by Christ Jesus.

This temple is eternal. It is magnificent because it is the work of Christ. And it is a temple that is ever growing—more and more believers are simply making it a more and more glorious temple.

Finally, this temple of believers is intended for one purpose—to reflect the *glory of God*. It is not intended to draw attention or praise to the believers, either individually or as a group, but, rather, to focus faith, hope, and love upon the One who created it—the Lord God Almighty!

Are you part of a body today that has been built upon the

"foundation of the apostles and prophets" with "Jesus Christ Himself being the chief cornerstone"?

Are you part of a body today that is focused entirely to bring glory to God?

The body of Christ as a whole most definitely is such a body. Our challenge as believers is to make certain that the body of believers with whom we worship on a local basis is 100 percent part of the greater body of Christ!

- *What new insights do you have into your identity as being part of a greater temple built to reflect the glory of God?*

  _____

  _____

- *In what ways are you feeling challenged in your spirit?*

  _____

  _____

What the Word Says	**What the Word Says to Me**
For you are the temple of the living God. As God has said: "I will dwell in them And walk among them. I will be their God, And they shall be My people." (2 Cor. 6:16)	_____ _____ _____ _____ _____ _____ _____
Do you not know that you are the temple of God and that the Spirit of God dwells in you? . . . For the temple of God is holy, which temple you are. (1 Cor. 3:16–17)	_____ _____ _____ _____ _____ _____

Many Functions, One Body

In being united to other believers in Christ's body, we do not lose our individual identity. Rather, we have the blessed opportunity to express our individual identity and gifts *in cooperation* with other believers. We are not all the same within the body of Christ—rather, we are united into one purpose.

Paul wrote about this very clearly to the Romans:

> For as we have many members in one body, but all the members do not have the same function, so we, being many, are one body in Christ, and individually members of one another. Having then gifts differing according to the grace that is given to us, let us use them: if prophecy, let us prophesy in proportion to our faith; or ministry, let us use it in our ministering; he who teaches, in teaching; he who exhorts, in exhortation; he who gives, with liberality; he who leads, with diligence; he who shows mercy, with cheerfulness. (Rom. 12:4–8)

We are to give our gifts in acts of ministry and open ourselves up to receiving the ministry gifts of other believers, so that we might be made whole *as a body* and so we might grow in our ability to love God and love others.

What the Word Says

There are diversities of gifts, but the same Spirit. There are differences of ministries, but the same Lord. And there are diversities of activities, but it is the same God who works all in all. (1 Cor. 12:4–6)

What the Word Says to Me

There is one body and one
Spirit, just as you were called
in one hope of your calling;
one Lord, one faith, one bap-
tism; one God and Father of
all, who is above all, and
through all, and in you all. But
to each one of us grace was
given according to the measure
of Christ's gift. (Eph. 4:4–7)

Christ—from whom the whole
body, joined and knit together
by what every joint supplies,
according to the effective
working by which every part
does its share, causes growth of
the body for the edifying of
itself in love. (Eph. 4:15–16)

Our Life As His Body

How can the body of Christ function if the body is scattered
and divided? How can the body of Christ function unless
believers come together periodically and worship the Lord and
engage in ministry one to the other?

Again and again, the writers of the New Testament called us
to be involved with one another. We are part of a living entity—
the body of Christ. We are intended to be in close relationship
and to function together as a whole. Read what the writers of
the Bible have said:

What the Word Says

What the Word Says to Me

And let us consider one
another in order to stir up love

and good works, not forsaking
the assembling of ourselves
together, as is the manner of
some, but exhorting one
another, and so much the
more as you see the Day
approaching. (Heb. 10:24–25)

Be filled with the Spirit, speaking to one another in psalms
and hymns and spiritual songs,
singing and making melody in
your heart to the Lord, giving
thanks always for all things to
God the Father in the name of
our Lord Jesus Christ, submit-
ting to one another in the fear
of God. (Eph. 5:18–21)

Confess your trespasses to one
another, and pray for one
another, that you may be
healed. (James 5:16)

Even so you, since you are
zealous for spiritual gifts, let it
be for the edification of the
church that you seek to excel.
(1 Cor. 14:12)

Therefore comfort each other
and edify one another.
(1 Thess. 5:11)

All that we do as members of Christ's body has a three-
fold purpose: to build up the body of Christ, to create a

sense of belonging for all believers, and to bring glory to the Lord.

If we truly have an identity as being part of the body of Christ, we will seek to function fully as part of the body. And in functioning as His body, we, in turn, grow in our own personal sense of belonging and of enjoying sweet reconciliation and fellowship with others.

- *What new insights do you have into your identity as a believer in Christ Jesus?*

  _____

  _____

- *How does it feel to belong, and to know that you belong fully?*

  _____

  _____

- *In what ways are you feeling challenged in your spirit?*

  _____

  _____

NINE

HOLY VESSEL FOR MINISTRY

As believers in Christ Jesus, we are members of a *living* body. In a very real and practical way, we are the "hands and feet" of the Lord on the earth today. Christ works through our hands to touch a sick person, clothe a naked person, and hand a cup of cold water to a thirsty person. Christ walks with our feet into areas of need. Christ speaks through our mouths His words of comfort and edification.

We have a great and glorious purpose on this earth—we are to be agents of God's love, ambassadors for Christ, the initiators of good works. We are to pour out our lives in service to others, just as Christ gave Himself for us.

Paul wrote to the Ephesians, "Be imitators of God as dear children. And walk in love, as Christ also has loved us and given Himself for us, an offering and a sacrifice to God for a sweet-smelling aroma" (Eph. 5:1–2).

While works can never save us, purchase our forgiveness, or qualify us to receive God's love, good works are the natural outcome of our salvation. Once we have been born again, our natural impulse is toward good works. As Paul also wrote, "For you were once darkness, but now you are light in the Lord. Walk as children of light (for the fruit of the Spirit is in all goodness, righteousness, and truth), finding out what is acceptable to the Lord" (Eph. 5:8–10).

Just as Christ Jesus walked this earth healing the sick and brokenhearted, preaching good tidings to the poor, proclaiming liberty to the captives, giving hope to the oppressed, and comforting those who mourn, so are we to follow in His footsteps and do the same. Jesus calls and commissions us to His ministry, just as He commissioned the disciples:

> And He called the twelve to Himself, and began to send them out two by two, and gave them power over unclean spirits . . . So they went out and preached that people should repent. And they cast out many demons, and anointed with oil many who were sick, and healed them. (Mark 6:7, 12–13)

What the Word Says	What the Word Says to Me
It is God who works in you both to will and to do for His good pleasure. (Phil. 2:13)	....
For to this you were called, because Christ also suffered for us, leaving us an example, that you should follow His steps. (1 Peter 2:21)	....

Created for Good Works

Paul wrote to the Ephesians that we have been "created in Christ Jesus for good works, which God prepared beforehand that we should walk in them" (Eph. 2:10).

God made you with a purpose in mind—He has had a plan for your life from before the foundation of the world, a plan that you are uniquely designed to implement and fulfill. The

Lord knows *precisely* the good works that you are not only capable of doing, but also those you will excel in doing and that will give you the greatest sense of satisfaction you can ever know.

> • *Have you had experiences in which you knew that you were doing precisely what God had created you to do?*

_____

_____

The characteristic that God attaches to your work is this: good. A "good work" is any work that reflects Jesus and that brings glory to God. *Good* is the same word that God used in evaluating each aspect of creation: "And God saw that it was good" (Gen. 1:10, 12, 18, 25).

The creative work of God is not finished. It is ongoing by the power of the Holy Spirit in your life and mine. God continues to shine light into darkness, to bring forth good out of evil, order out of confusion, and purpose out of things that seem meaningless. One of the best-known verses in all the Bible declares this: "All things work together for good to those who love God, to those who are the called according to His purpose" (Rom. 8:28). No matter what happens to us or around us, the Holy Spirit is capable of producing a "good work" in us and through us!

> • *How do you feel knowing that you were created in Christ Jesus for good works?*
> I want my Heavnly Father to be proud

What the Word Says

You will know them by their fruits. Do men gather grapes

What the Word Says to Me

_____

_____

from thornbushes or figs from thistles? Even so, every good tree bears good fruit, but a bad tree bears bad fruit. A good tree cannot bear bad fruit, nor can a bad tree bear good fruit . . . Therefore by their fruits you will know them. (Matt. 7:16–18, 20)

what is my fruits?

Be doers of the word, and not hearers only, deceiving yourselves. For if anyone is a hearer of the word and not a doer, he is like a man observing his natural face in a mirror; for he observes himself, goes away, and immediately forgets what kind of man he was. But he who looks into the perfect law of liberty and continues in it, and is not a forgetful hearer but a doer of the work, this one will be blessed in what he does. (James 1:22–25)

Lord please give me ears to hear!

Then God saw everything that He had made, and indeed it was very good. (Gen. 1:31)

He made me + He made our Son.

No Room for an Inferiority Complex

So many Christians seem to say about themselves, "I'm not capable" when it comes to ministry. The fact is, none of us are capable in and of ourselves. But equally true is this fact: with Christ, all things are possible. As Paul said to the Philippians,

"I can do all things through Christ who strengthens me" (Phil. 4:13).

God supplies to us what we are lacking and what we need. When we are weak, He gives us the strength to be strong. When we are without resources, He supplies the resources. When we are without courage, He gives us the ability to endure and to be bold. Again and again in the Bible we have examples of those who *could not* in their own ability, but who *could* as they received the strength of the Lord.

Paul wrote about a painful "thorn in the flesh" that the Lord did not remove from his life even though he had prayed repeatedly that it be removed. He told the Corinthians how the Lord had said to him, "My grace is sufficient for you, for My strength is made perfect in weakness." Paul concluded, "Therefore most gladly I will rather boast in my infirmities, that the power of Christ may rest upon me. Therefore I take pleasure in infirmities, in reproaches, in needs, in persecutions, in distresses, for Christ's sake. For when I am weak, then I am strong" (2 Cor. 12:9–10).

What the Word Says

And God is able to make all grace abound toward you, that you, always having all sufficiency in all things, may have an abundance for every good work. (2 Cor. 9:8)

But may the God of all grace, who called us to His eternal glory by Christ Jesus . . . perfect, establish, strengthen, and settle you. (1 Peter 5:10)

I bow my knees to the Father of our Lord Jesus Christ . . .

What the Word Says to Me

----

that He would grant you, according to the riches of His glory, to be strengthened with might through His Spirit in the inner man. (Eph. 3:14, 16)

Our Identity As His Witnesses

Not only are we created for good works, but we are called to be Christ's witnesses. We are to proclaim the good news of His death and resurrection—and to be bold in telling others about God's love, mercy, grace, and free offer of forgiveness and eternal life. We have a "good message" to accompany our "good works"!

When Peter and John were put in prison, and then were called before the religious leaders in Jerusalem and threatened for proclaiming that Jesus was the Christ, Peter and John said, "We cannot but speak the things which we have seen and heard" (Acts 4:20). Peter and John were released with further threats, and they returned to their fellow believers. After they had told all that had happened to them, Peter and John and the disciples prayed this: "Now, Lord, look on their threats, and grant to Your servants that with all boldness they may speak Your word" (Acts 4:29). What was the result? "They spoke the word of God with boldness" and the "multitude of those who believed were of one heart and one soul" (Acts 4:31–32).

- *How do you feel about God's call to you to be His bold witness?* 1st Thought not me. That's meant for Dear 12 t
  2nd - Pray thought heart of willingness to share.

- *In what ways are you feeling challenged in your spirit?*

What the Word Says	What the Word Says to Me
[Jesus said,] "Go therefore and make disciples of all the nations, baptizing them in the name of the Father and of the Son and of the Holy Spirit, teaching them to observe all things that I have commanded you; and lo, I am with you always, even to the end of the age." (Matt. 28:19–20)	Humble myself let God do what He will though me.
[Jesus said,] "Go into all the world and preach the gospel to every creature." (Mark 16:15)	
[Jesus said,] "You shall be witnesses to Me in Jerusalem, and in all Judea and Samaria, and to the end of the earth." (Acts 1:8)	

Our Identity As His Ambassadors

In doing good works, and in proclaiming the "good news" of Christ, we are God's ambassadors. As Paul wrote to the Corinthians, "We are ambassadors for Christ, as though God were pleading through us" (2 Cor. 5:20). Our identity is as citizens of heaven, sojourning on this earth in temporary "tents"—our physical bodies. We are "fellow citizens with the saints" who have gone before us (see Eph. 2:19). Our true home is in heaven.

When we truly see ourselves as citizens of an everlasting kingdom—only temporarily on this earth to speak the "good news" of Christ as often as we can to as many as we can, and to do the good works that the Holy Spirit leads us to do—we will have a new perspective on our possessions, our commitments and agendas, and our use of time and resources. Our priorities will change. No longer will we see ourselves as having to strive to accomplish man-made goals on this earth; no longer will we cling to material things; no longer will we feel the need to make alliances so we can "get ahead" and achieve fame and power in the eyes of the world.

When we have a firm identity that we are a citizen of heaven, an ambassador for Christ on this earth, and a temporary resident of earth on a "mission" for God, we will seek to make the most of our earthly time and resources for eternal reward!

What the Word Says

We do not lose heart. Even though our outward man is perishing, yet the inward man is being renewed day by day. For our light affliction, which is but for a moment, is working for us a far more exceeding and eternal weight of glory, while we do not look at the things which are seen, but at the things which are not seen. For the things which are seen are temporary, but the things which are not seen are eternal. For we know that if our earthly house, this tent, is destroyed, we have a building from God, a house not made with hands, eternal in the heavens . . . For we who are in this tent groan,

What the Word Says to Me

----

being burdened, not because we want to be unclothed, but further clothed, that mortality may be swallowed up by life. Now He who has prepared us for this very thing is God, who also has given us the Spirit as a guarantee. So we are always confident, knowing that while we are at home in the body we are absent from the Lord . . . We are confident, yes, well pleased rather to be absent from the body and to be present with the Lord.
(2 Cor. 4:16–5:1, 4–6, 8)

[Jesus said,] "Do not lay up for yourselves treasures on earth, where moth and rust destroy and where thieves break in and steal; but lay up for yourselves treasures in heaven, where neither moth nor rust destroys and where thieves do not break in and steal. For where your treasure is, there your heart will be also." (Matt. 6:19–21)

Do you truly see yourself today as a vessel of God intended for His purposes of ministry on this earth—purposes that involve the doing of good works and the proclaiming of the good news? Ask the Lord to help you see yourself as He sees you. So many Christians seem to think that once they are saved, the rest of their lives is a long, slow slide through life until they land in eternity. Not so! We have work to do and a message to proclaim. And today is the day for doing what God has called us to do!

- *What new insights do you have into your identity as a believer in Christ Jesus?*

  _____

  _____

- *In what ways are you feeling challenged in your spirit?*

  _____

  _____

TEN

GOD'S
MASTERPIECE

A re you aware that you are God's masterpiece?

The apostle Paul wrote to the Ephesians, "We are His workmanship" (Eph. 2:10). The word *workmanship* has been translated also as "masterpiece." We are God's supreme "work in progress"—a work that will culminate in perfection.

A masterpiece is a work of notable excellence. From the first chapter of the Bible we see that God considered man to be the crowning achievement of His creation. Of all God's creatures, only man was made in the image of God—only man was made capable of spiritual growth and development, of reasoning, of faith, of learning concepts and principles, of making sound decisions and wise judgments, of planning for a future and remembering the details of the past. God breathed into man His own breath, His essence, His presence. God gave man a will with which to discern good from evil and to choose between them.

Whether you see yourself as a piece of a mess or a masterpiece makes a great difference. If you have an identity based upon a self-image that you are worthless, without potential and without any hope of excellence, you are likely to give up, become dejected, and become "sick of life." On the other hand, if you have an identity based upon a self-image that you are a masterpiece in the making, with vast potential for excellence, you are going to have hope, enthusiasm for life, and a desire to pursue all that God has for you!

> • *How do you feel about your own identity as a "master-piece"—the workmanship of God?*

_____

_____

God's Plan: Our Perfection

As we have stated repeatedly in this Bible study, we are believers *in Christ*. Christ Himself is our identity. Here is what Paul said about Christ: "He [Christ] is the image of the invisible God" (Col. 1:15).

Jesus Christ was the appearance of God in flesh form—God incarnate—so that we might see the perfection of God in a human likeness to which we could relate fully.

If we are *in Christ*, we also are to reflect the perfection of God in human form. As Paul also stated, "For it pleased the Father that in Him all the fullness should dwell" (Col. 1:19).

Jesus Christ was the *begotten* Son of God. From the moment of His birth He was a perfect reflection of God's nature.

We are the *born-again, in-the-process-of-becoming-perfect* children of God. From the moment of our spiritual rebirth, we are indwelled by the Holy Spirit and set on a path of growing up in the fullness of a perfect reflection of Christ's nature.

Our future *is* that we will be like Christ. We will be perfect, whole, complete—just as He is perfect, whole, and complete.

Throughout the New Testament we find numerous references that point to God's plan for our lives as being a plan of perfection, wholeness, completion, and fullness. As you read through the verses below, note the theme of God's bringing us to a perfect reflection of Himself.

What the Word Says

He who has begun a good work in you will complete it until the day of Jesus Christ. (Phil. 1:6)

[Jesus said,] "Therefore you shall be perfect, just as your Father in heaven is perfect." (Matt. 5:48)

[Jesus prayed,] "I in them, and You in Me; that they may be made perfect in one." (John 17:23)

Become complete. Be of good comfort, be of one mind, live in peace; and the God of love and peace will be with you. (2 Cor. 13:11)

All Scripture is given by inspiration of God, and is profitable for doctrine, for reproof, for correction, for instruction in righteousness, that the man of God may be complete, thoroughly equipped for every good work. (2 Tim. 3:16–17)

Now may the God of peace who brought up our Lord Jesus from the dead, that great Shepherd of the sheep,

What the Word Says to Me

through the blood of the everlasting covenant, make you
complete in every good work
to do His will, working in you
what is well pleasing in His
sight, through Jesus Christ, to
whom be glory forever and
ever. (Heb. 13:20–21)

Just as Christ also loved the
church and gave Himself for
her, that He might sanctify and
cleanse her with the washing of
water by the word, that He
might present her to Himself a
glorious church, not having
spot or wrinkle or any such
thing, but that she should be
holy and without blemish.
(Eph. 5:25–27)

What a glorious future lies ahead for us! But note, if you will, that in each of the verses listed above, it is God who does the sanctifying, cleansing, and perfecting work in us—by His Word and by His presence, He is the One who *makes* us whole. Our perfection is not something we can achieve or should strive to achieve. Our perfection is not of our own doing—we are *His* workmanship.

- *What new insights do you have into your identity as God's masterpiece?*

The Perfecting Process

The process of our perfection may at times be painful. It is God who chisels us, sands us, makes us, molds us. It is God who sometimes chooses to bring us into difficult times and situations so that we might deepen our reliance upon Him and grow in our relationship with Him. We are clay in His hands:

> The word which came to Jeremiah from the LORD, saying: "Arise and go down to the potter's house, and there I will cause you to hear My words." Then I went down to the potter's house, and there he was, making something at the wheel. And the vessel that he made of clay was marred in the hand of the potter; so he made it again into another vessel, as it seemed good to the potter to make.
>
> Then the word of the LORD came to me, saying: "O house of Israel, can I not do with you as this potter?" says the LORD. "Look, as the clay is in the potter's hand, so are you in My hand." (Jer. 18:1–6)

- *Have you had an experience in which you felt the Lord was "remaking" you on His potter's wheel?*

_____

_____

- *What emotions do you have as you reflect upon what it means to be "remade" in the hands of God?*

_____

_____

A Cleansing Process

Through the years, I have had the opportunity to visit some of the famous art galleries and museums in the world, and as I do, I look for the paintings that are my favorites. In one museum, I noticed that a particular painting was missing, and

I asked a guide if it had been loaned or sold to another museum. He responded, "No, it is out being cleaned." From time to time, God removes us from the spotlight so that He might cleanse something from our lives. Always, His perfecting work is a work of removing dross or impurities from our lives so that we might more perfectly reflect Him.

What the Word Says	What the Word Says to Me
Therefore the Lord says . . . I will turn My hand against you, And thoroughly purge away your dross, And take away all your alloy . . . Afterward you shall be called the city of righteousness, the faithful city. (Isa. 1:24–26)	
He is like a refiner's fire And like launderers' soap. He will sit as a refiner and a purifier of silver; He will purify the sons of Levi, And purge them as gold and silver, That they may offer to the Lord An offering in righteousness. (Mal. 3:2–3)	
Jesus Christ, who gave Himself for us, that He might redeem us from every lawless deed and purify for Himself His own	

special people, zealous for
good works. (Titus 2:13–14)

Believing God for Perfection

If God alone does the work of perfecting us—of making us, remaking us, refining us—what is our part? Our part is to *receive by faith what it is that God says He is doing in our lives!*

We are to take God at His Word and trust Him to do His work in us, opening ourselves to His work, inviting His work in us, and believing that even though we may not see all of the results we would like to see *when* we would like to see them, *God is at work!* He is always behind the scenes of our lives, turning all things toward an eternal benefit for us. We are His workmanship. He never removes His grace from our lives. He never withdraws or takes His hand off of us. We are always in His everlasting arms.

What God begins, God completes.

What the Word Says

Looking unto Jesus, the author
and finisher of our faith. (Heb.
12:2)

Commit your way to the
LORD,
Trust also in Him,
And He shall bring it to pass.
He shall bring forth your
righteousness as the light.
(Ps. 37:5–6)

Trust in the LORD with all
your heart,
And lean not on your own
understanding;

What the Word Says to Me

In all your ways acknowledge
Him,
And He shall direct your
paths. (Prov. 3:5–6)

Taking God at His Word

It is God who says today that the moment you receive Jesus Christ as your Savior, you are *in Christ*. It is God who says that He chose you, He loves you, He has redeemed you from the bondage of sin, and that He has forgiven you and changed your sin nature. It is God who declares that you are His heir, an enlightened saint with the mind of Christ, a member of the body of Christ, and a holy vessel in His hands. It is God who declares that you are His masterpiece.

The real question facing us today is this: Will you believe what God says about you? Will you take Him at His word, by faith, and trust Him to do His work in you?

- *What new insights do you have into your identity as a believer in Christ Jesus?*

- *In what ways are you feeling challenged in your spirit?*

BELIEVE FOR GOD'S BEST

We each have a choice on a daily basis as to what we will think about ourselves and how we, therefore, will behave.

We can say, "I am never going to amount to anything." Or we can say, "I am the workmanship of God, His masterpiece in the making. I have an excellent future of perfection in Christ Jesus!"

We can say, "Nobody loves me. I must be unworthy of love." Or we can say, "I am the beloved child of God."

We can say, "I am worthless, of no value, a nothing and a nobody." Or we can say, "God sent His only Son to die on the cross for me—He considers me worthy of His Son's death!"

We can say, "I'm poor and stupid." Or we can say, "I am an heir of God, a joint-heir with Christ Jesus, and I have been given all spiritual blessings *with wisdom and understanding*. I have the mind of Christ."

We can say, "I don't belong anywhere. I'm an outcast." Or we can say, "I am a member of Christ's own body."

We can say, "I can't do anything for God." Or we can say, "I am a holy vessel whom God desires to use for good works and to proclaim the good news."

The choice is ours.

What is it that *you* will choose as your identity today? Will it be the identity based upon your feelings, or will the identity that God has declared be the truth of your life?